Former corporate lawyer, co-founder of a successful software company and technology investor, David Gillespie is the best-selling author of the *Sweet Poison* books, *Big Fat Lies*, *Free Schools*, *Toxic Oil*, *Eat Real Food*, *The Eat Real Food Cookbook*, *Taming Toxic People*, *Teen Brain*, *The Good Fat Guide* and *Brain Reset*. He lives in Brisbane with his wife and six children.

Also by David Gillespie

The *Sweet Poison* books
Big Fat Lies
Free Schools
Toxic Oil
Eat Real Food
The Eat Real Food Cookbook
Taming Toxic People
Teen Brain
The Good Fat Guide
Brain Reset

David Gillespie

Toxic at Work

MACMILLAN
Pan Macmillan Australia

Pan Macmillan acknowledges the Traditional Custodians of Country throughout Australia and their connections to lands, waters and communities. We pay our respect to Elders past and present and extend that respect to all Aboriginal and Torres Strait Islander peoples today. We honour more than sixty thousand years of storytelling, art and culture.

First published 2023 in Macmillan by Pan Macmillan Australia Pty Ltd
1 Market Street, Sydney, New South Wales, Australia, 2000

A catalogue record for this book is available from the National Library of Australia

Typeset in 11/18.5 pt Sabon LT Std by Midland Typesetters, Australia
Printed by IVE

The paper in this book is FSC® certified. FSC® promotes environmentally responsible, socially beneficial and economically viable management of the world's forests.

To Lizzie, and to our six kids at the start of their working lives: Anthony, James, Gwen, Adam, Bib and Fin.

Contents

Introduction

Is your boss a psycho? How about the bloke in the office next door? Is the woman who owns your business one? Are some of your customers psychos? What about your suppliers? There is a one in twenty chance – at least – that there is psycho in your workplace. You may think that working in a caring profession (nursing, teaching), or a not-for-profit, or a business with a save-the-world mission statement insulates you against psychos. It does not. They are everywhere.

I'm not talking about people with psychosis, a mental health condition that means they suffer from delusions and paranoia. I am talking about psychopaths, people with no empathy, who do not care if you live or die as long as you benefit them. The term 'psychopath' may conjure up images of notorious killers and vicious criminals, but the reality is more subtle and insidious.

Psychopaths can occupy any role in your workplace, from your boss to your colleagues, suppliers or clients. Their presence is not only difficult to detect but also has far-reaching consequences for your personal and professional life, as well as the organisation you work for.

You may instinctively resist the idea of labelling someone a psychopath. You won't want to use this term because you think that psychopaths are murderers and rapists. You won't want to call them a psychopath because, if you have bought this book, you are a normal person (someone with empathy), and empathetic people are pre-programmed to trust others. But this reluctance is precisely the vulnerability psychopaths exploit.

You won't recognise them as psychopaths because they share many of the same traits as the people we adulate – rock stars, Instagram celebrities, people who have publicly accrued wealth and success. You won't recognise them as psychopaths because HR and psychologists and other self-helpers use a dizzying array of labels to describe what is essentially psychopathic behaviour. They might talk about workplace bullies, narcissists, socio-paths, manipulators, dark empaths or just bad bosses. But they are all describing a person with a single point of failure: a failure of empathy.

You also won't recognise them as psychopaths because they will have charmed the pants off you, at least initially. Over time, the psychopath's true nature may gradually emerge through an array of destructive behaviours. They start to micromanage your work. They take credit for your successes and blame you for their failures. They impose an atmosphere of secrecy. They make sure no-one knows the whole story about anything. They create cliques of insiders and outsiders, which they use to bully and humiliate individuals while the group looks the other way. All of this undermines your confidence and destroys your trust in your colleagues. At first, you might dismiss their actions as symptoms of stress, busyness or anxiety. You might even blame yourself, constantly striving to improve in the hope of appeasing them. However, the damage they inflict can be both personally devastating, and terminal to the team, organisation or business you work for, as they erode trust and teamwork – two critical components of collective success and survival.

In this book, we will embark on a journey to uncover the hidden world of workplace psychopaths. We will explore their tactics, their ability to thrive, and the strategies you can use to protect yourself and your organisation. We will dissect the typical behaviours of psychopaths and show you how to spot them and manage their influence.

We'll take a close look at the lives of some well-known leaders like 'Chainsaw' Al Dunlap, Donald Trump and Steve Jobs to show how a lack of empathy becomes obvious once you know what to look for. We'll go to the movies with Ricky Gervais to see how gullible the world looks to a psychopath. I'll introduce you to the work of Kent Kiehl, a psychologist who has devoted his life to scanning the brains of psychopaths and used that work to show why it is impossible to threaten a psychopath. We'll also explore the Mendota Juvenile Treatment Center in Wisconsin, a prison where the 'guards' are psychologists who have shown how psychopaths can be controlled. And I'll take you into the odd academic world of game theory, to look at whether psychopaths make different decisions to the rest of us when asked to imagine a life-or-death scenario.

While all of that will give us a taste of how they behave, in order to really understand a psychopath, we need to see the world through their eyes. To do that we'll enter the fictional universe of Stephanie, Alice, Scott and Jasmine to see a typical workplace through the eyes of a psychopath and those around them. We'll look at the same set of events from the perspective of the psychopath, their primary victim, bystanders and their employers. This will help us to really understand how the world looks to the truly empathy-free and we will see the enormous damage that perspective does to others. We'll see how the psychopath completely destroys the lives of almost everyone they meet without having any grand plan other than making sure they are slightly better off today than they were yesterday. And we'll see how some co-workers fall victim to this, how one avoids it and how their boss is oblivious to it.

At its core, the best defence against a psychopath in the work-place is a well-run company that can efficiently contain or expel them. By understanding the risks posed by psychopaths and learning how to respond to them, you can not only safeguard your personal wellbeing but also ensure the long-term success and stability of the organisation you work for. So let us begin this voyage together, as we navigate the intricate landscape of the chameleons among us – the hidden psychopaths in your workplace.

1

Chameleons among us

PSYCHOPATHS THROUGHOUT HISTORY

In August 1941, J Edgar Hoover, the first director of the fledgling Federal Bureau of Investigation, was told the Japanese intended to attack Pearl Harbor by the end of the year. He was provided with two convincing pieces of evidence that showed exactly how the attack would take place. But J Edgar didn't trust the person giving him this information, so instead of passing it on to the US military, he chose to boast about his forensic capabilities in discovering the evidence by passing only some of it on. Unfortunately he omitted the information about Pearl Harbor. Four months later, at 7.48 am on Sunday, 7 December, 353 aircraft launched from six Imperial Japanese Navy aircraft carriers attacked the US fleet at anchor in Hawaii's Pearl Harbor. Ninety minutes later, 2403 American servicemen had been killed, 21 US Navy ships had been lost or badly damaged and over 300 combat aircraft had been destroyed or damaged.

The person who provided Hoover with the crucial intelligence was Duško Popov, a Yugoslav-born double agent working for both British and German intelligence. Popov had managed to infiltrate the highest ranks of the Abwehr, the German military intelligence, and provided valuable information to the British throughout the war. He had earned the codename 'Tricycle' because of his involvement in a three-way espionage network.

Popov had been given the task of gathering information on the US Navy's capabilities and defences, particularly in Hawaii. The Germans shared this intelligence with their Japanese allies, who were preparing for a surprise attack on the US Pacific Fleet. Popov passed on the information he had collected to his British handlers, who promptly alerted the Americans, and a clandestine interview with the FBI was arranged.

One of the first things Popov told the FBI was that Pearl Harbor would be attacked by the end of the year. He had two pieces of evidence to back up the claim. The first was a communique from the German Air Attaché in Tokyo reporting on a trip he had undertaken with Japanese naval officers to Taranto, Italy.

The communique revealed that the Japanese officers had been intensely interested in gathering every possible detail of the November 1940 British attack which destroyed the battle effectiveness of the Italian navy. The British aircraft carrier, *Illustrious*, with twenty-one antiquated Swordfish biplane torpedo bombers, had devastated the Italian naval fleet at anchor in the Bay of Taranto. Up until that point naval orthodoxy was that aerial torpedoes could not be used in shallow water. But the British had found a way to make sure they could, and the result was spectacular, effectively eliminating the Italian navy as a threat in the Mediterranean.

The Taranto attack had been front-page news in the US in November 1940, with both the *New York Times* and the *Washington Post* running lengthy analyses of the devastating effect of air power on the Italian fleet at anchor. The US Chief of Naval Operations took the threat seriously and wrote to the commander at Pearl Harbor, Admiral Richardson, referring to Taranto and asking him to install torpedo nets. Richardson declined, citing the improbability of an attack and the shallowness of the harbour. Over the subsequent months, US naval attachés stationed aboard British ships continued to report advances in torpedo technology which meant that shallow water was no longer an effective defence. Those reports made it to the Office of Naval Intelligence in the US, but their recommendations were never implemented.

The second piece of evidence was a set of questions from Japanese intelligence about Pearl Harbor, which the Abwehr had provided Popov. The Japanese wanted detailed information about dredging, the depth of the water, the existence and location of torpedo nets and the location and carrying capacity of the three airfields near the US Navy base. The Germans had concluded, and told Popov, that Japan intended to replicate a shallow-water aerial torpedo attack on the anchored US fleet at Pearl.

Popov was known for his playboy lifestyle, which contributed to his success as a double agent. Born into a wealthy and influential Yugoslav family, Popov enjoyed the finer things in life and had a taste for fast cars and faster women. His charisma and charm made it easy for him to socialise with high society and navigate elite circles, which proved beneficial for his espionage work.

Popov's playboy persona also played a role in inspiring Ian Fleming's iconic character, James Bond. In early 1941, Fleming, then working for the British Secret Service, observed Popov at a casino in neutral Portugal, where he was seen skilfully working the roulette tables, mingling with informants and charming elegant women. This encounter likely influenced Fleming's portrayal of Bond in his first novel, *Casino Royale*.

Hoover didn't like Popov's playboy, Bond-like lifestyle and he didn't trust him, despite MI6 vouching for his bona fides, so Hoover didn't pass the warning on. He did tell the military that he had interviewed Popov, but focused on the fact that Popov had used the Germans' newly invented microdot technology to store the Japanese questions rather than on what Popov had said or what the questions were about. Hoover didn't mention that Popov had been asked to provide detailed information about the defences at Pearl Harbor.

Had Hoover passed on the intelligence, it may well have converted the possibility of attack to certainty in the minds of the navy decision-makers. It was a tragic and expensive failure of trust. Why would someone so thoroughly distrust another person that they would risk the destruction of the US fleet and the death of thousands of servicemen? Why would they control the flow of information? Why would they choose to boast about themselves rather than warn the navy?

1

After recovering from testicular cancer, then virtually unknown American road-racing cyclist Lance Armstrong won seven consecutive Tours de France between 1999 and 2005. Prior to this spectacular feat he had only ever won single stages of the 21-stage race; once in 1993 when he didn't finish the race, and again in 1995 when he finished 36th overall. Winning the race at all, let alone winning seven in a row, certainly attracted attention. Armstrong was an American hero. He was a cancer survivor, who had started a foundation for cancer sufferers, and he was a charming and engaging ambassador for the sport. But that mask eventually slipped.

In October 2012, the US Anti-Doping Agency (USADA) charged Armstrong with running a massive doping ring and with the use of performance-enhancing drugs. The report concluded that Armstrong was engaged in 'the most sophisticated, professionalized and successful doping program that sport has ever seen'. Armstrong denied the allegations but did not contest the charges. After they were confirmed by the International Cycling Union, he was stripped of all wins since 1998, including the bronze medal he won at the Sydney 2000 Olympics, and was permanently banned from the sport. In a 2013 interview with Oprah Winfrey, Armstrong admitted to the doping charges. He had spent most of the previous fifteen years ruining the lives of anyone who suggested he was doping.

When the team masseuse, Emma O'Reilly, told journalist David Walsh that Armstrong was a drug cheat in 2003, Armstrong publicly branded her an 'alcoholic whore' and sued her. The pressure of the lawsuit and the associated publicity ended her marriage. When fellow cyclist and previous Tour de France winner Greg Lamond expressed doubts about Armstrong being clean in 2001, Armstrong told him he could find ten people who would testify that Lamond was a drug cheat. Lamond's wife later told a court that Armstrong offered one of Lamond's teammates $300,000 to say he had seen Lamond using drugs.

According to Armstrong's fellow cyclist and best friend Frankie Andreu and Frankie's wife Betsy, Armstrong told his oncologist that he was doping when he was receiving cancer treatment. Betsy says she was there when Armstrong said it. When Betsy passed this on to David Walsh for use in his 2004 book *LA Confidential*, she faced constant public vilification from Armstrong, who called her a 'crazy bitch' and a 'psycho' and sued her for libel. In 2011, Olympic gold medal cyclist and Armstrong's former teammate, Tyler Hamilton, admitted to doping and accused Armstrong of doing the same. When Hamilton became a witness in a Federal case against Armstrong for defrauding the US Postal Service – the sponsor of Armstrong's team – he said Armstrong accosted him in a bar and threatened, 'When you're on the witness stand, we are going to fucking tear you apart. You are going to look like a fucking idiot. I'm going to make your life a living . . . fucking hell.'

When Winfrey raised his long history of lawsuits, vilification and intimidation, Armstrong explained that all the menacing, bullying and domination was just him trying to control the narrative. He was just trying to 'perpetuate the story and hide the truth'. The damage this did to others did not appear to cross his mind at all. In a 2015 BBC interview Armstrong admitted that, given the chance, 'he would probably do it again'. Armstrong had spent most of his career lying about doping. When those lies were challenged, he viciously attacked and often destroyed those he knew were telling the truth. And he apparently felt no remorse for any of it. Why would someone have such a callous disregard for the truth? Why would they not care what it did to others? And why would they feel absolutely no remorse for destroying so many lives and reputations?

2

This is a book about an evolutionary throwback that still lives among us. You might know them as micromanagers, bullies, narcissists, Machiavellian manipulators, antisocial personalities, toxic people or sociopaths. I prefer to call them psychopaths. But whatever you call them, they are not human – at least in the sense that they are not like the rest of us. Evolution has passed them by. A critical piece of wiring is missing. They are version 1.0 humans living among version 2.0 humans. Version 2.0 humans have the wiring for empathy. Psychopaths don't.

Hoover and Armstrong's stories are examples of a failure of empathy. To be clear, empathy is not the same as sympathy, and we didn't evolve empathy to be nice – that's just a happy side effect. Empathy is what allows us to trust and care about other humans. It means we are capable of cooperating with others. And when we cooperate, instead of an individual fighting a tiger in the jungle, we are a team of specialists working together. We are no longer meat on feet – together, we are the apex predator. Humans with empathy default to trusting other people and considering the impact of our actions on them.

The famous American billionaire investment guru Warren Buffett once said, 'Trust is like the air we breathe. When it is present, nobody really notices. But when it's absent, everybody notices.' A co-worker who, for example, refuses to share their details of a contact for a potential client is telling you they don't trust you or the organisation. They are afraid you'll take the credit for the interaction without acknowledging their role, or perhaps they fear that you will take over the relationship and cut them out. This lack of trust harms you, your co-worker and the organisation. When this is compounded over hundreds or even thousands of daily interactions, organisational capability will be seriously impaired.

If you can trust your team to give credit where it is due, then you will share valuable information and nobody will waste time chasing the limelight. A team of people who trust each other will resolve inevitable conflicts without them becoming permanent sources of paranoia. In high-trust organisations, employees have high levels of autonomy, and according to workplace research this enhances motivation and performance. This should not be surprising. If you know your boss trusts you to get your work done, you won't spend time justifying your decisions. A trusted team will identify areas for productivity improvement. A micro-managed team will keep their ideas to themselves for fear of being labelled a troublemaker. If you trust the other members of your team to play their part, you won't spend time checking that they are pulling their weight. Trust allows us to get on with the job.

A person with properly functioning empathy would have trusted Duško Popov. Yes, he was a double agent, but MI6 disclosed this, had introduced him to the FBI and trusted him. He had brought Hoover valuable information which confirmed the navy's existing intelligence. Had that information been passed on, the US Navy may well have moved the fleet to sea, or installed torpedo nets. The Japanese might have given up their plan, or the results at least would have been dramatically less damaging. Yet Hoover prioritised telling people how smart he was by decoding the Germans' new microdot technology over sharing what Popov had revealed. No normal person faced with a choice between the possible death of thousands and a small benefit to themselves would make the choice that Hoover did. But Hoover was not a normal person. He was a paranoid narcissist with an insatiable need for flattering publicity. Importantly, he didn't believe in trust. As one of his aides once said, 'Hoover didn't trust anyone he didn't have something on.'

Hoover believed that the only reason anyone did anything was because they were coerced. He famously had a file on everyone of influence. And the leverage those files provided kept Hoover in his position as director of the FBI from the Bureau's inception in 1924 until he died in office in 1972, at the age of 77. Even John F Kennedy, who hated Hoover with a passion, reappointed him as director because he knew Hoover had amassed detailed files on his sexual indiscretions. When Richard Nixon tried to get rid of Hoover in a private meeting, Hoover came out of the meeting not only with his job secure, but also with an increase in budget for the FBI. But he had nothing on Popov, had no way to control him, and therefore assumed he was doing exactly what Hoover would do – lie.

In a 2020 ESPN documentary Betsy Andreu said of Lance Armstrong, 'I don't think to this day he realises the damage he's done to people; I don't think he cares.' A person with functioning empathy would not have destroyed his friends' lives to maintain what he knew to be a lie. And if they did, a person with functioning empathy would be remorseful for the damage they caused and seek to make amends. Without empathy, they are unable to really put themselves in another's shoes. They are unable to feel the pain they cause. It's not that they don't care, it's that they can't.

Hoover held a nation to ransom to maintain his position. No cost, not even Pearl Harbor, was too great. Armstrong caused brutal and lasting damage to the lives of those around him to maintain his status as the world's greatest road-racing cyclist. Many view these behaviours as evil personified. However, in order to successfully survive an encounter with a psychopath, we need to view their actions through a different lens.

3

I want you to peer inside the mind of a psychopath. I want you to see the world through their eyes. Try thinking of other humans like they are a cheap chair. Their sole purpose is to support you. You have absolutely no concern for the chair's welfare. You do not care what the chair thinks of you. As soon as the chair stops providing the support you need, you throw it away and get another. If you need to break it up for firewood, you do so without hesitation. There are no exceptions. Your mother, your wife, your friends, and strangers are all the same. You will keep them around as long as they are useful, and dispose of them when they are not.

You do not think of yourself as evil for feeling this way. You are not impaired in any way by a sense of conscience. You do not feel remorse or shame. You act only in your best interests, and do whatever it takes to benefit you. Any harm that causes to others only concerns you if it inconveniences you. You are aware that other people don't think this way, but you see their altruistic behaviour as a weakness you can exploit. You live in a dog-eat-dog world where most of the other dogs are on moral leashes. This gives you a distinct advantage.

When a psychopath is caught doing something wrong, they cannot be shamed into feeling remorse. They are incapable of remorse, and would commit the same act again in the same circumstances. We struggle to understand that way of thinking because we have automated concern for our fellow humans. We can be evil, but for us, crossing that line is a conscious decision, and we feel remorse if we do. For a psychopath there are no lines. Everything is an option, and asking them to feel shame or remorse is like asking a blind man to see the colour blue.

Lacking the wiring for empathy doesn't just mean psychopaths operate without regard for others. It also disables the ability to learn from mistakes. This is probably why Lance Armstrong said he would do it all again given the chance. And had Hoover been asked, I doubt he would have changed anything either. Because empathy is biochemistry – the wiring used for it is integral to many functions of our brain, including memory, impulse control, emotional responses and even our ability to detect minute differences in smells, sounds and colours.

At least one in twenty people are psychopaths. You will encounter psychopaths at work, in relationships, at your local sporting club and in your family. This is a book about under-standing how the psychopathic mind works, and how to use that understanding to survive your encounter with a psychopath. And let's face it, in a workplace, survival is often the only choice. Most of us need our jobs. We can't just up and quit because the boss or our colleague is a psychopath – at least not straight away. We need to extricate ourselves in a controlled fashion that minimises harm to us and our careers.

It is not useful to think of a psychopath as being evil. When we do that, we superimpose a layer of morality on their thinking which simply does not exist. We assume limits which are simply not there. We make assumptions about what motivates them and how they behave which will be dangerously wrong. When a psychopath doesn't pass on information that could save thousands of lives, we look for complex explanations rather than accepting the obvious – Hoover didn't trust someone he couldn't blackmail. When a psychopath will trade your life for a minuscule advantage to them, that is all that is going on. It is not part of some grand plan, it is just them choosing the option that, at that moment in time, benefits them more. When you're late for work because the kids wouldn't get ready for school and Janice says she will cover for you, then tells the boss you were late because you were hungover, it's because she saw an opportunity to make herself look good and make you look bad. She didn't give it any more thought than that. There was no great plot against you, just a microscopic advantage to her. Yes, you will hate her for that, but she doesn't care. That's like expecting her to care what her office chair thinks of her recent weight gain. Your feelings just don't matter.

To help us understand this fundamental difference in the way psychopaths think, I'm going to take you inside the minds of two Olympic coaches who approached their teams in fundamentally different ways to see how empathy affected the way they played. We're going to dig deep into why we (most of us) have empathy in the first place and why that didn't stop the COVID toilet paper panic when it should have. I'm going to take you into the strange world of game theory and prisoner's dilemmas to demonstrate how scientists have distilled the way most people think into a simple game called Tit for Tat. And together we're going to discover how that simple game accurately describes the way most of us operate in a world where trust is a fundamental requirement.

I'm going to introduce you to Lee Holloway, the man responsible for much of the software that secures the internet, who suffered from a type of dementia that destroyed his capacity for empathy. We'll look at how paracetamol is degrading the empathy of anyone who consumes it regularly. And I'll explain how studies of people like Lee have helped us understand what is different about the brains of psychopaths. You'll also meet Hervey Cleckley, the psychiatrist who in 1941 first described psychopathy as a mask of sanity and used Scarlett O'Hara in *Gone with the Wind* as an example.

The point of all this is to answer four simple questions that lie at the heart of every interaction we have with psychopaths. What is wrong with this person? Why are they doing this to me? How do I make it stop? And how do I avoid this ever happening again?

2

The evolution of empathy

COOPERATION, TRUST AND THE TRAGEDY OF THE COMMONS

Humans are easy prey in a world full of far more powerful predators. But we are more likely to survive if we stick together. Groups that cooperate do better than groups that don't. We can only cooperate if we trust the other people in our group. We can only trust other people if we take account of their needs, and if we are confident they will do the same for us. Trust-powered cooperation is critical to our survival as a species, so we have evolved a hard-wired mechanism to ensure we trust each other. We call that mechanism empathy.

One Friday afternoon in late February 1980, twenty clean-cut no-name boys snatched an Olympic ice hockey gold medal from the reigning Olympic and world champions. It was a modern-day David and Goliath moment, forever immortalised as the

Miracle on Ice. Twenty-four years later, the US Olympic men's basketball team missed out on a gold medal they should have won easily. Why did the ice hockey no-names succeed where the basketball Dream Team failed? The answer is simple: a champion team will always beat a team of champions.

The Soviet ice hockey team were the heavy favourites to take gold in 1980. They had won five of the six preceding Winter Olympics, and 27 of the 29 Olympic matches they had played since 1960. They had not lost a single game in Olympic play since 1968.

The Soviet team included 28-year-old Vladislav Tretiak, generally regarded as one of the greatest goaltenders in the history of the sport. He was part of the gold medal-winning Soviet teams at the 1972 and 1976 Olympics. The captain of both those teams, 35-year-old Boris Mikhailov, was also there again in 1980. Mikhailov had won eight World Championships between 1969 and 1979. He was playing alongside 32-year-old Valeri Kharlamov, generally regarded as one of the best forwards the game has ever produced, and 33-year-old centre Vladimir Petrov. Like Tretiak, Mikhailov and Kharlamov, Petrov had won gold in '72 and '76, and had a mountain of other international gold medals to his name.

Even the younger players in the team came with impressive resumes. Defenceman Viacheslav Fetisov was just 21, but he had already won two consecutive gold medals at the World Junior Championships and one at the 1978 World Championships. Another rookie was twenty-year-old left winger Vladimir 'The Tank' Krutov, generally regarded as one of the best wingers of the eighties. He would go on to win gold at the 1984 and 1988 Olympics, and five World Championship golds from 1981 to 1989.

Similarly, 21-year-old right winger Sergei Makarov came into the 1980 Olympics team with a swag of junior gold medals to his name, and would become one of the greats of the sport. This was truly a team of superstars. It was little wonder they were expected to win gold, and win it easily.

With an average age of just 21, the US team challenging this team of Soviet legends was the youngest at the Olympics and the youngest in US National Team history. There was just one member of the fifth-placed 1976 team in the 1980 roster, 25-year-old left wing, Buzz Schneider. The rest were kids. College all-stars, for sure – fifteen of the twenty had already been promised National Hockey League contracts – but kids nonetheless.

Their coach was 42-year-old former national player Herb Brooks. Born and raised in St Paul, Minnesota, Brooks had won the 1955 Minnesota State Championships as part of his high school team and played for the University of Minnesota from 1955 to 1959. He had been cut from the gold medal-winning 1960 US Olympic team just a week before the Games, but went on to be part of the 1964 and 1968 Olympic teams, placing fifth and sixth respectively. In 1970, he retired from playing and took up a coaching position at his alma mater, the University of Minnesota, coaching the Gophers to National Championship wins in 1974, 1975 and 1979. Shortly after the 1979 win, he was offered the role of Olympic coach.

Nine of the final twenty-man squad had played under Brooks at the University of Minnesota, and four were from Minnesota's arch rival, Boston University. They were clean-cut – Brooks insisted on no facial hair – and according to commentators at the time, the team looked like a bunch of fifteen-year-old boys lining up against the men from the rest of the world.

Six months earlier, at the US Olympic ice hockey tryout camp in Colorado Springs, Brooks had whittled 68 candidates down to 26 with the help of a 300-question psychology quiz he'd had specially created. He knew that everyone in that final 68 could play ice hockey, and play it well. The test was designed to find open-minded people. Brooks didn't want 'the ignorant people, the self-centred people, the people who don't want to expand their thoughts'. In other words, he didn't want the kind of player that made up 90 per cent of the National Hockey League at the time. He didn't want players whose only focus was using Olympic selection to get the attention of the NHL scouts. He wanted players who could learn how to play together as a team, not kids chasing big money contracts and individual glory.

This ethos carried through everything he did with the team. They lived, trained and played together for seven months. Even though he knew many of the young players well – he had, after all, been the coach of half the team for years – he intentionally distanced himself from them. He was brutal in his conditioning drills.

A famous scene from the 1981 movie *Miracle on Ice* perfectly captures Herb's approach to the team. By all accounts, the scene faithfully recreates the way Herb coached. The friendly match against a Junior A Norway team was one of the first in a 63-game series of invitationals to prepare the team for the Olympics. The game ended in a 3–3 tie. Herb was not happy.

As the team came off the ice, he told them to get back out there and line up on the base line. They would be doing the dreaded sprints subsequently christened 'Herbies'. Netballers know the same drill as 'suicides'. A Herbie consists of sprinting from the base line to the blue line, then back, then to the halfway line, then back, then to the further blue line, then back, then the full court. In the film Kurt Russell, playing Herb, memorably says, 'You think you can win on talent alone? Gentlemen, you don't have enough talent to win on talent alone.' Then, after a few more Herbies, he tells them, 'When you pull on that jersey, you represent yourself and your teammates. The name on the front [USA] is a helluva lot more important than the one on the back. Get that through your head.' Brooks kept them doing Herbies for over an hour, to the astonishment of the slowly dwindling crowd. The players were on the brink of total exhaustion before he relented. The next night, they played the same Norwegian team again. This time the US won 9–0.

Another example of Herb's approach came just before the Olympics began. Brooks threatened to cut the captain because he was becoming complacent in lead-up matches. The team got the message – no-one was a star, no-one was indispensable. The team bonded like troops under fire. They came to the Olympics united and determined to show Herb they could win. Herb was tough on the physical conditioning, but he was convinced the only way to win against the best was to play as a team, to play for each other rather than for themselves.

They entered the competition ranked seventh of the eight nations competing. Their first game was against second-ranked Sweden. After the first period the Swedes were up 1–0. Brooks was in a rage in the break. They were one period into their Olympic campaign and just one goal down and their coach was freaking out. It got so bad that the captain, 23-year-old Mike Eruzione, threw Brooks out of the locker room so the team could focus. They were determined to show Brooks they had what it took. They tied the game, which was all they needed to do in the early rounds. Two nights later they thrashed the third seed, Czechoslovakia, 7–3 and the world started to pay attention. Then came Norway, Romania and West Germany. The superpowers of hockey were falling like ninepins to this bunch of nobodies. Brooks later attributed their frequent come-from-behind wins to their ability to retain discipline and teamwork.

Brooks infuriated the IOC by refusing to have players present at the post-match press conferences. It was mandatory to send three players, but Herb didn't want any stars in his team. When the press started to complain, saying Brooks was hogging the limelight, he sent his assistant coach instead. There were still no players. There were no names. There were no stars. The players were anonymous, and they kept winning against the odds.

The game against the Soviet superstars was hotly anticipated, but no-one dared hope the unlikely nobodies had any real chance – not even the team themselves. The match was set against a backdrop of extreme international tension between the US and the USSR. The Cold War was at its peak, US embassy staff were being held hostage in Iran, Russia had just invaded Afghanistan, and the US had just announced it would be boycotting the Moscow Summer Olympics in retaliation. Both countries needed a win.

The game was, unexpectedly, a nail-biter. Twice, the Soviets would score only for the US to get the equaliser. With 11 minutes and 21 seconds left in the game the US equalised at 3–3. And then the impossible happened. With exactly 10 minutes to go, the US team captain Eruzione scored. And that's where the score stayed. There was no equaliser this time. Ten minutes later, the boys next door had pulled off the most unlikely win in hockey history. As *Sports Illustrated* writer Ed Swift wrote about the team when they were awarded the coveted Sportsman of the Year 1980, 'the whole was greater than the sum of its parts by a mile'.

How did they snatch victory from the Soviets? They valued working together more than individual glory. By hook or by crook, they had discovered the leverage of cooperation.

1

The 2004 US Olympic basketball team was coached by 63-year-old Larry Brown, fresh from his NBA win with the Detroit Pistons, and was stuffed with stars and future stars of the professional game. Powerhouse rookies LeBron James, Dwyane Wade and Carmelo Anthony shared the bench with legends of the game like Stephon Marbury, Tim Duncan and Allen Iverson.

The US had not lost a single game in Olympic competition since the introduction of professional players at the 1992 Olympics. They had brought home three consecutive gold medals. It was the US first and daylight second. So, when the superstar line-up was announced for the 2004 Games, the result was considered a foregone conclusion. The US had picked the twelve best players in the NBA, the world's preeminent competition – what chance did the rest of the world have?

Quite a good chance, as it turned out. The US didn't even make it to the gold medal round, and just managed to scrape out a win for bronze against Lithuania. They lost three matches from the eight they played at the 2004 Games, the most lost by a US men's team before or since, and more than the total of all matches lost to that point by all US Olympic basketball teams combined.

Coach Brown was not a fan of the roster from the get-go, and he let everybody know it. He preferred veteran players. He didn't want young players like LeBron James, Dwyane Wade and Carmelo Anthony in the mix, and he publicly criticised the team make-up. This meant these young superstars of the game rode the pine for most of the competition. But his dislike of the players didn't end there.

Coach Brown had worked with team captain Allen Iverson previously, at the Philadelphia 76ers, and their relationship had been famously dysfunctional. No-one told Allen Iverson how to play ball or whether to turn up to practice. Both were convinced they were the top dog, and neither was prepared to concede any ground. Brown frequently aired his grievances about Iverson to the press, and Allen was not shy in returning fire. The result was frequent duels by media, and the 76ers were sinking fast when Brown jumped ship and hitched his wagon to the upwardly mobile Detroit team.

All-Star and All-NBA Superstar Stephon Marbury hated Brown's rigid adherence to what he viewed as an inflexible and old-fashioned playing style. He told reporters at the Olympics that the coach wasn't letting the team just play. When word got back to Brown, he tried to get Marbury booted from the team.

Marbury later described the Olympic campaign as the 'worst 38 days' of his life. He said being in that team was unbearable. No-one wanted to play for Brown, and the energy was terrible.

The 'team' was a group of very talented individuals, but it was not a team. The players selected for the Olympic 'Dream Team' had all become individually rich by making sure they featured in the highlight reels aired on ESPN. To star in those reels, a player had to have flashy individual plays. No-one makes the highlight reel for a team play that keeps possession and gets the ball to the hoop.

These players were in it for themselves, working for a coach who openly criticised them, and it showed on court. When Argentina crushed the US team's chance to play in the gold medal playoff, NBC Olympics commentator Mike Breen said it best when he observed, 'The game is still played at its best when five players are working together, and the United States just didn't have enough of those moments, where Argentina it was like five guys on a string.'

Why did the ice hockey team succeed where the basketball team failed? The answer is that success in team sports is often dependent on giving up individual stardom so the team can succeed.

2

Team success is based on avoiding something economists call the tragedy of the commons. The theory first emerged in the early nineteenth century when English economist William Lloyd observed the behaviour of farmers sharing common grazing land in Great Britain – the 'Common'. Lloyd wrote that if herders did not work together to preserve the Common, then self-interested individual herders would overgraze and destroy the community asset. Those farmers would benefit in the short term, but would suffer with the rest once the asset was destroyed. We have all recently seen a tragedy of the commons play out in our local supermarket.

When the COVID-19 lockdowns affected several countries in 2020, many of us discovered that our local supermarket had run out of toilet paper. People were panic buying what they perceived to be a critical resource. As the first shortages appeared, those who had been holding back in the interests of the common good abandoned that stance, so as not to miss out. When the tragedy of the commons begins to unfold, the end comes very quickly as the cascade of self-interest turns from a snowball into an avalanche. No-one knew how long the lockdowns might last, and the one thing people were not prepared to live without was toilet paper. Authorities had not anticipated this demand for TP, and the market was wholly unregulated. There was nothing to stop a self-interested individual buying as much as they could afford – so they did.

Eventually, buying limits were introduced and the highly prized resource began to reappear on the shelves. Policing is one way of preserving the commons, but this is not always possible. Sometimes the commons rapidly collapses without warning. Sometimes it's just not feasible at all. Having the umpires hand out penalties for showboating might change player behaviour, but it is unlikely to become part of team sport anytime soon. And often, there is no umpire or police force. There is no-one with the authority to enforce rules preserving the common asset. This is, of course, why on a world scale, commons such as clean air, fresh water, well-stocked fisheries and global temperatures are unable to be preserved. There are no world police to protect the commons.

So how did the ice hockey team succeed without a police force keeping their self-interest in check? They did it because long ago, humans evolved a solution to the tragedy of the commons. That solution is trust. Teams that trust each other perform better than those who don't. The success of the team despite other people's doubts became more important to them than their individual success. They were playing for each other more than they were playing for themselves. As Mark Pavelich, the player who set up the winning goal in the game subsequently christened the Miracle on Ice, said at the time, 'We wanted to win it for ourselves.' Note he said 'ourselves' not 'myself.' They wanted to win for each other.

3

The power in teamwork comes from the distribution of workload. If everyone contributes equally, the sum of their output will be greater than the individual parts. But how can you be sure the other members of the group will play their part? How do you know they won't run when the going gets tough, or stab you in the back when it comes to sharing the rewards? The answer is simple: you can't be sure. You just have to trust them. For a group to become a team, each member of the group will need to trust that the other members will play their part. Trust is a sort of team lubricant. If we can trust our teammates, we don't need to invest energy in doing their job, or checking that they are doing it right. We can just focus on our job and trust them to do theirs.

Imagine you have a serious medical condition that requires surgery. Money is no object, so you can fly in the best heart surgeon in the country. Alternatively, you can go with the cardiac surgery team in your local hospital. What would you do? Most of us would probably choose the superstar over the team – and we'd be wrong.

In 2006, Robert Huckman and Gary Pisano from Harvard Business School tested this scenario with real-world data. They looked at outcomes from over 38,000 procedures performed by 203 cardiac surgeons at 43 hospitals in Pennsylvania. They found that when a surgeon was working at his usual hospital with his usual team, his success rates increased incrementally over time. But when that same surgeon left their team and became a visiting specialist at another hospital, their success rate returned to baseline. Huckman and Pisano concluded that star performance is not portable. It was the team that was delivering the star outcomes, not the individual.

And it's not just doctors who get better results in teams than alone. Robert Huckman later went on to look at teams of software developers. He found that the number of times the developers had previously worked with each other was a better predictor of project success and timely delivery than the total experience of the team members. Since then, teams in many industries have been closely studied and most research arrives at the same conclusion. If you assemble a competent team who are prepared to work together, the team will outperform any single member working alone.

This makes intuitive sense from an evolutionary perspective. When it comes to outcompeting other apex predators, humans don't have much going for them. We don't have fangs, venom or horns, and we're not particularly strong. If we find ourselves going one on one with a lion, crocodile, shark or elephant, we are very likely to come off second best. Humans who have the ability to work together as a team clearly have a survival advantage. But being a team means more than just standing near each other. A group of humans is not necessarily a team of humans. Both the 2004 basketball team and the 1980 hockey team were groups, but only one was a true team.

Why do we trust other people? The answer is that in most situations, it works out better for us if we do. This is particularly true if we know we will see the other person again.

4

In 1950, two mathematicians working for a newly formed military strategy think tank, Rand Corporation, came up with a simple thought experiment that revolutionised research on why and when we trust others.

The prisoner's dilemma is deceptively simple. Two criminals – let's call them Albert and Bob – are arrested, and accused of committing a crime. They are put in separate interview rooms with no way of communicating with each other. The police admit to each offender that they don't have enough evidence to convict either of them with the primary offence, which carries a sentence of three years, but they do have enough to convict them each of a minor offence which will put them away for one year.

The police offer each offender a deal. If they give a sworn statement that the other person was solely responsible for the crime, they will walk free. But there's a catch. If Albert and Bob both betray each other, they will both go to prison for two years.

If they both say nothing, then they each go to jail for one year. But if one gives a statement while the other keeps quiet, then the one who betrayed the other walks free and the one who stayed quiet gets three years in jail.

		Albert	
		Confess	Don't confess
Bob	Confess	Both get two years	Albert free Bob gets three years
	Don't confess	Bob free Albert gets three years	Both get one year

The prisoner's dilemma

What should Albert do? The best outcome for them both is to keep quiet, and each get a year in prison, but can Albert trust Bob? Will Bob throw him under the bus to walk free? Should Albert assume he will, and get his statement in? Evolutionary theory says that the only rational decision is that Albert should squeal. Evolution is intrinsically competitive. Species are in a constant battle for shared resources, and the winner takes all. Self-interest is the rational outcome of evolutionary competition. If they do pursue self-interest, each prisoner will confess and they will both go to prison for two years, rather than risk going away for three years. They will have sacrificed the Commons – in this case, the potential for a one-year sentence for both of them – for the certainty of avoiding a three-year sentence for themselves.

Self-interest is the only strategy a rational player can follow that maximises his benefit without regard to what the other person does. If they rat the other out, it is a sure thing that they will not go to prison for three years, and they may get off altogether. But if they both act out of self-interest, as rational actors surely should, the tragedy of the commons will kick in and they will both be worse off. There is no place in evolutionary theory for altruism, giving up a potential benefit for the common good.

The researchers tested this theory in the real world by getting Rand secretaries to play a version of the game that didn't involve prison time. In that version of the game, each player can choose to pay a fixed amount (say $1), or not pay. Neither knows what the other has done until the round is over. If you pay, the other person gets $3 and vice versa. If you both pay, you both end up with an extra $2, being the $3 you receive less the $1 you paid. If you pay but they don't, you are out a dollar and they are up $3, and vice versa. If neither of you pay, you both get nothing.

		Albert	
		Cooperate (pay $1)	Cheat (don't pay)
Bob	Cooperate (pay $1)	Both get $2	Albert gets $3 Bob gets nothing
	Cheat (don't pay)	Bob gets $3 Albert gets nothing	Both get nothing

The monetary version of the prisoner's dilemma

Just as with the prisoner's dilemma, self-interest says the secretaries should not pay. If the other player pays you get $3, and if they don't you don't lose anything. But that is not what happened. The secretaries tended to cooperate. In other words, both paid even though that meant potentially sacrificing a greater reward (by cheating on the other person). This was a theoretically irrational strategy. It relied on trusting the other person to do the right thing, and not cheat.

In May 2023, a Brisbane radio station, KIIS FM, held a competition called 'KIIS the Cash'. Ten contestants were required to kiss a Perspex box containing $20,000 cash for as long as they could. The last person kissing the cash won it. Except there was a twist. On the fourth day, there were just two contestants left, a heavily pregnant mother of young children and another woman recovering from ovarian cancer. Both had spent three days side by side with their lips pressed against the cash. And both said they desperately needed the money. Neither would give up. In a shock announcement, the radio station introduced a prisoner's dilemma to solve the impasse. The women were told that on the count of three they would need to step back from the cash or stay attached. If both stepped back, they would each get $10,000. If one stepped back and the other didn't, then the one still kissing the cash would get $20,000 and the other would get nothing. If neither stepped back, the cash would be given to a randomly selected member of the audience. What would you do? The rational thing to do would be to stay attached knowing most people are likely to play nice and step back. You would win $20,000 and everyone would think you were horrible, but you would win $20,000. But that didn't happen. Just like the Rand secretaries, the contestants chose to cooperate. With tears streaming down their faces, they both stepped back on the count of three. They knew it was possible the other person would not. They knew the other person might put their need for the money above their reputation or the needs of a stranger they had met just three days ago. But they trusted each other to do the right thing.

Why did real humans defy the competitive theory of evolution and cooperate to preserve the commons? Because these real people knew each other, and cared about their reputations. Cheating would affect those reputations and impact their relationships.

5

Even if the participants don't know each other, or they are just bots in a computer game, real-world reputation can be incorporated in the prisoner's dilemma model by simply having two strangers play the monetary version of the game more than once. With each successive round, they learn more about the other person. If person B cheats in the first round, should person A cheat in the second round or give person B a second chance? This so-called iterated prisoner's dilemma has formed the basis for thousands of experiments in human trust.

In the early 1980s, Robert Axelrod, a political scientist from the University of Michigan, organised a tournament for academics studying the iterated prisoner's dilemma. Research teams from all over the world were invited to submit their solutions. He wanted to know what the best strategy was. Should a player cooperate all the time, or every second time, or only in response to cooperation from the other player, or only when the other player cheats or . . .

you get the idea. He asked the participating researchers to come up with the strategy that earned their player the most when playing consecutive rounds. The strategies were then pitted against each other over 200 iterations using a tournament format in a computer simulation of the game.

The winner was Anatol Rapoport, a retired mathematical psychologist living in Canada. Rapoport created a very simple strategy which he called 'Tit for Tat'. In Tit for Tat, the player always pays on the first round. After that, the Tit for Tat player always does what the other player did on the previous round. If the other player cheats, the Tit for Tat player cheats. If they cooperate, then so does the Tit for Tat player. Tit for Tat is a very simple mirroring strategy. You start out being 'nice', but if the other player cheats, you retaliate until they are nice again. You can be mean, but you are prepared to let bygones be bygones.

Tit for Tat won convincingly against all the other algorithms tried. When Axelrod published the results, a second tournament was organised to see if anyone could come up with a strategy that could beat it. They couldn't. All manner of complex strategies were tried, and none succeeded. JOSS, for example, was nice most of the time but tried to get away with a sneaky cheat every now and then. And DOWNING had a complex decision tree which tried to predict the other player's behaviour by analysing the previous moves. Tit for Tat won convincingly again, even when the competition knew the opponent would be playing Tit for Tat.

Evolution works by preserving species with successful life strategies and eliminating those with less successful ones. In order to more closely mimic evolution, Axelrod then organised a further 'ecological' tournament. In this version, a number of players, say ten, pursuing each strategy started the round and played against all other players. At the end of a round the most successful strategy received extra players at the expense of the least successful strategy. Again, Tit for Tat came to dominate the population of players. If you want to see this played out visually, check out the 'Evolution of Trust,' Nicky Case's online simulation, a magnificently well put together illustration of Axelrod's work.

Why does Tit for Tat work so well? The strategy just reflects our behaviour back at us. The only way we can succeed long term is to treat others the way we want to be treated. It seems trusting other people and having others trust us is mostly made up of mirroring their behaviour towards us.

6

Humans are a dominant predator because we have managed to solve the tragedy of the commons and work together in cooperative, interdependent teams. The reason Tit for Tat was so successful is because it hit upon a central truth about how to organise groups of strangers with no incentive to assist each other.

Mirroring behaviour is part of almost every religion and philosophy humans have ever written down. This action is so central to humanity, it has been dubbed the Golden Rule. The Christian New Testament expresses the Golden Rule as 'You shall love your neighbour as yourself.' But this is not the whole story. Turning the other cheek is a laudable principle to aim for, but the Old Testament recognises the reality of human interactions. We start out nice, but will retaliate if cheated. Old Testament books tell us to take an eye for an eye and a tooth for a tooth. While that might sound brutal, it was intended as a way of keeping retaliation in check. It should be read as take *only* one eye for an eye – nothing more. This was an expression of the foundational Roman legal principle of reciprocal justice, designed to restrict compensation to the size of the loss. In other words, we should be nice, but if we are wronged, our retaliation should be limited to the amount of damage sustained and no more. If you lose an eye, you take an eye in retaliation. You don't kill the man and hold a grudge against his family for generations. Vendettas destroy the commons, but like-for-like retaliation preserves it by keeping selfish behaviour in check.

Tit for Tat is a simple scientific model that makes reliable predictions about how real groups of strangers will behave. But it is just a model. Real life is quite a bit more complicated. In real life, people can sometimes be deceptive or manipulative, and are honest in some situations while cheating in others. Sometimes it's about knowing your teammate will pass to you if you're in a better position, rather than attempt to hog the glory for himself. Sometimes, it's about a surgeon trusting the anaesthetist to know when the patient is in trouble and trusting the surgical nurse to close properly after he finishes. Life is messy, and rarely as simple as 'the other person put in a dollar so I get three'.

The Golden Rule provides an insight into our core operating system, but navigating the nuances of real human behaviour requires a more sophisticated approach. The Golden Rule doesn't always get the right answer, but it gets it right enough of the time to ensure continued survival of the species.

We've been writing the Golden Rule down for as long as we've been writing anything down – about 5000 years – but we've been a separate species for around a quarter of a million years. So where did it come from? The Bible says the Lord told us about 5000 years ago, but that seems unlikely, given that we'd been managing to self-organise for 250,000 years prior to that. The reality is that we have evolved a unique ability to automatically predict the behaviour and sense the emotions of other humans. We evolved empathy, the critical precursor to trust.

In real life, we are not sitting in another room with no information about the person we are being asked to trust. We can usually see them and the way they behave, and they can see us. We automatically begin to make assessments about the degree to which we can trust them. Imagine you are running a sports club that allows casual members to show up and play each week, as long as they pay in cash on the day. Phillip shows up without any cash, but wants to play. He says he will pay next week. Do you trust him? Your answer will largely depend on what you subconsciously observe about Phillip, and many of those criteria will be things you might not even admit to yourself, or even knowingly observe.

How do we know if we can trust another person, and how do they know they can trust us? We use a kind of sixth sense called empathy. The Golden Rule is an expression of empathy. It requires us to consider the feelings and needs of others in order to treat them as we would want to be treated. Empathy is uniquely human, but it, and therefore the Golden Rule, evolved from mirroring, a system that animals in groups developed for instantaneous communication.

If you belong to a species that relies on safety in numbers as your primary defence against predators, there is an obvious evolution-ary advantage to reacting quickly to potential danger. It would be even more advantageous if you didn't need to actually see the danger yourself, but could automatically react if another member of your group did. If the whole group can react to danger as they would if they had personally spotted it, then the group has the leverage of many eyes. Everyone is on the lookout and no-one is on the lookout. This means the whole group is able to continue feeding, mating and protecting the young, knowing that if anyone spots danger, everyone spots danger. No long-winded explana-tions are needed. When Fred is startled, you are startled. It may seem like magic, but researchers are starting to uncover the solid biological foundations for that kind of behaviour.

This almost telepathic capability uses specialist structures called mirror neurons. When one member of the group detects a threat, they might change body posture, facial expression or vocalisation. For example, they might suddenly freeze when they notice danger. Before the other members of the group have time to think about it, their mirror neurons have picked up on the change in the first member's movement and posture and caused them to react, together, as if they had spotted the danger themselves.

Mirror neurons were first discovered in the early 1990s by a team at the University of Parma in Italy, led by neurophysiologist Giacomo Rizzolatti. As with many great scientific discoveries, it was all a bit of an accident. The team had implanted measuring nodes in motor neuron parts of the brains of macaque monkeys, with the aim of measuring whether those neurons fired differently when the monkey was handling different objects. The team began recording the firing patterns while giving the monkeys different things to hold. But then they noticed something odd. The wired-up monkeys' neurons fired in exactly the same way when they noticed a researcher pick up the object as they did when the monkey picked up the object themselves. The patterns were identical. And this wasn't by chance. The neuron that fired when a researcher picked up a peanut was identical to the one that fired when the monkey did it. A different neuron fired when the researcher ate the peanut, and that same neuron fired when the monkey ate it. Neurons in the monkeys' brains were behaving like the monkey was performing the action, when they were actually watching a human do it.

Rizzolatti followed up this research with human studies in 1995. These were less precise – rather than digging around in people's brains, they measured muscle signals transmitted when a muscle is about to move. Nevertheless, these studies showed the same thing happening. When a participant observed a researcher grasping an object, their muscles transmitted the same signals as when they grasped the object themselves. Subsequent human studies using functional MRI technology have shown the same thing over and over again. Our motor neurons mirror things we see other people do.

The late Tommy Lasorda, two-time World Series manager of the Los Angeles Dodgers Major League Baseball team, reckoned, 'Hitting is contagious. One guy starts hitting well, the other guys are gonna catch on.' Ask any baseball coach and they will tell you the same thing. It's a truism of the game: when a batter starts getting hits, the following batters are more likely to get hits too. This was put to the test by Rob Gray from the University of Birmingham and Sian Beilock from the University of Chicago in the early 2000s. They gathered twelve experienced and twelve novice college baseball players, then ran them through a series of standardised batting experiments with and without watching someone else getting a hit first. Before they watched a successful hit, the experienced players needed to receive an average of two pitches before getting a hit and the inexperienced players needed to receive 3.5. But when both had the opportunity to see a successful hit before they stepped up to bat, those averages dropped to 1.25 and 2.5 respectively. Major League statistics back up those results. A 2012 study of batting averages since 1945 confirmed that batters following a batter who hits are around 11 per cent more likely to get a hit than they otherwise would be. This observation holds true even after adjusting for batting order, pitching changes and overall team skill.

It appears that mirror neurons allow us to run simulations of an action without needing to actually perform the action. They let us learn by watching rather than just by doing. But that's not all. More recent research has established that they help us make predictions as well.

In one study, researchers measured mirror neuron activity in macaques in response to two actions. A researcher would pick up an apple and either put it to her mouth or place it in a cup. The mirror neurons were measured after the first part of the action, picking the apple up, but before it was clear whether it would then go up to the mouth or in the cup. The mirror neurons only fired when the apple went up to the mouth. Something about the way the researcher moved had tipped off her intentions to the ever-observant mirror neurons.

Very recent research with baseball players – yes, there is a lot of money in baseball – has confirmed that humans are capable of the same magic trick.

A batter has 0.4 seconds of ball flight time to complete a hitting action that takes the best players in the world at least 0.3 seconds, so accurate pitch prediction is mandatory if you want to play elite baseball. Functional MRI results for a group of professional baseball players were compared to those of non-players while watching pitches. They were asked to predict whether the pitch would be a strike or a 'ball'. Unsurprisingly, just as with Rob Gray's studies, the professionals were better at this than the non-players, but all the participants engaged their mirror neuron networks. Looking at just the professionals, the pitchers engaged mirror neurons in the motor complex – they were paying attention to and learning the motor steps in pitching. But in the batters, there was higher engagement in mirror neurons associated with simulation and perception. Batters' mirror neurons fired more when they saw a ball that was a strike. They might not know why they knew it was a strike, but their mirror neurons had correctly picked it.

The value of this automated sub-second, unconscious reaction feature extends beyond baseball players and monkeys. Any group of animals is more likely to survive if it can transmit data from individual to individual at the speed of light using microscopic unconscious changes in vocalisation, expressions and posture. We just have to see an action to replicate it using the mirror neurons. We don't need to think about what we are seeing or process a response. The neuron reacts instantly. The mirror neuron system is billions of times faster than communicating any other way, and likely to be the difference between being a tiger's next meal and living to tell the tale.

Our mirror network is active all the time. We are seeing every change of body position, every facial expression, every eye movement and much, much more than we consciously notice. Just like the monkeys who can predict whether an apple will be eaten or put in a cup, or the batters who can see a strike that no-one else can, everything we see is being copied and analysed by our mirror network. It is being used to constantly make predictions about the people around us.

Mirror neurons are like little empathy superheroes in our brains, helping us feel what others feel. When we see someone in pain, these neurons make us wince too. They help us connect with others on a deeper level. But there's a catch. To get the most out of them, we have to interact with other people in person. When we interact online, our mirror neurons don't work as well. For example, when we chat with co-workers on a text-based platform like Slack, we miss out on those visual cues that help us understand each other better. We can't tell if the other person is smiling, frowning or wincing, so our empathy superheroes stay on the sidelines.

Video calls, like Zoom, are a step up, but they have their own issues. We only see people's heads, not their full bodies, which can make it harder to pick up on important non-verbal cues. And let's not even get started on slow internet connections and buffering. Another problem is that we often lose the important little sounds people make when we're communicating, like laughter or sighs. Anyone who's given a presentation on Zoom knows the feeling. It's way harder to gauge how you're doing when everyone's microphones are muted. In person, we can hear and see people's reactions, which helps our mirror neurons work their magic.

So, while online interactions are super convenient, they can sometimes make it harder for us to really connect with others. Our empathy superheroes – our mirror neurons – just don't have the same opportunities to perform as they do in person. In March 2020, most of the business world undertook an involuntary experiment in remote work, thanks to COVID. Although few of us would have chosen it, the experience has provided valuable insights into how much we need our mirror neurons to work together effectively. During 2021, Microsoft, the creator of one of the biggest corporate video conferencing tools, Teams, conducted over 50 studies on the impact of remote working.

They found that a full year of remote work seriously affected our connections with co-workers. People reported feeling more and more disconnected, and when the Microsoft researchers looked at the data from billions of Outlook emails and Teams meetings, there was an obvious pattern: working from home had made our networks smaller. When the pandemic first hit, the researchers found that people actually interacted more with their close work buddies, but over time they let those more casual connections fade away. As we all locked down at home, we focused on staying in touch with the people we were used to seeing all the time, and those 'once in a while' relationships just didn't make the cut. In short, employees became more isolated, with groups sticking to their own little bubbles. Even worse, the research showed that a year into this remote work lifestyle, even those tight-knit team interactions began to dwindle. So not only did we lose touch with our more distant work connections, but our close relationships also took a hit. If we don't see our co-workers, we disable, or at least impair, one of our most critical communications tools, and a critical foundation piece to how we cooperate in large groups.

The mirror neuron is an effective light-speed communications network for animals in groups, but when it comes to social behaviour it is just the first step. Schools of fish and flocks of starlings transmit and copy movement signals using mirror neurons, but there is no evidence that they are using that information to behave socially. They are not solving the tragedy of the commons to preserve resources; they are reacting from moment to moment based on each other's behaviour. Humans do much more than merely mirror each other's behaviour.

Imagine you're in the crowd at the cricket when Ricky Ponting smacks a six in your direction. The bloke in front of you doesn't see it coming and catches it with his noggin. Automatically you recoil as if you were the one who got hit by the ball. Or perhaps you see a friend sniff an unfamiliar food and look like they're about to bring up their breakfast, and suddenly you feel a bit queasy too. We've all been there. We've seen someone experience something and felt almost like it happened to us. Multiple studies have shown conclusively that the same thing occurs with facial expressions showing pain or disgust. And this is more than mere imitation. We actually appear to feel the pain or disgust being expressed. When we recoil at someone copping a cricket ball in the skull, we actually feel it. When we retch at the disgust shown by our dodgy-food sniffing friend, we really do feel their disgust.

How is this possible? How do we feel what another person is feeling? The answer is that humans have evolved von Economo neurons, a brain structure that creates a simulation of another person's emotions based on the feedback from the mirror neurons. (More on these later.) We don't sympathise with someone in pain, we empathise with them. We actually feel their pain, their sorrow, their happiness, their disgust and every other emotion as if it were really happening to us. And, importantly, we automatically use that empathy in our decisions about how to behave.

8

In 2015, Keren Haroush from Stanford University teamed up with Ziv Williams from Harvard to determine if rhesus monkeys solved the iterated prisoner's dilemma in the same way as humans. The monkeys were playing for drops of juice rather than money, but the logic of the game was the same. The researchers found that if the monkeys could see each other, but not the choice the other monkey made, then they tended to follow a Tit for Tat strategy and performed as well as humans. If, however, they were placed in separate rooms, the tragedy of the commons killed their results as both tried to cheat. For those monkeys, social cooperation only continued for as long as they could see the other monkey.

Humans, on the other hand, continue to cooperate even if they cannot see the other person. This is why humans can cooperate with humans they have never met and can't see.

You may never have met the people in the London office, but you trust them to help you with your project. You are unlikely to have met the person who builds the products you are buying from Spain, but you trust that they will meet your needs. Social cooperation with strangers enables us to leverage the skills of those strangers to accomplish far more than any individual could achieve. Imagine how much less you would achieve if you had to travel to London to check the work of your colleagues. Imagine if you had to travel to Spain to watch the worker build your product. Cooperation is a superpower that separates humans from even our closest relatives in the animal kingdom.

The big advantage of doing this experiment with monkeys rather than humans was that it was possible to monitor very precisely what was going on at the neural level. The researchers found that distinct areas of the anterior cingulate cortex (ACC), the part of the brain used to process emotional responses, were being used to calculate predictions about what the other monkey might do. One part performed calculations based on receiving the juice reward and another part performed calculations based on social self-interest – how their behaviour might be perceived by the other monkey.

The researchers were able to measure exactly how much calculation was being performed by each part of the ACC during each part of the experiment. Before the monkey made its choice, it spent twice as much computing power on its own choice than on considering how it might look to the other monkey. After a choice was made but before the monkey knew what the other monkey had chosen, however, the brain entered a predictive phase. During that phase, total processing doubled and the emphasis switched from calculations about juice self-interest to calculations about social self-interest.

The moderation of self-interest by social calculations significantly improved the chances that the monkeys would cooperate and solve the tragedy of the commons. Haroush and Williams also found that disrupting these calculations with an electrical current caused the monkeys to default to the tragedy of the commons as they both tried to cheat.

Most animals spend a significant amount of their time seeking food while trying to avoid *being* food. They share a dopamine-powered reward and alarm system that drives the seeking or running away behaviour. We describe the feelings that motivate that system as basic emotions. Animals, including us, feel four basic emotions: fear, aggression, happiness and sadness. Fear makes us run away from danger. Aggression makes us fight for rewards. We are happy when we get the reward or avoid the danger, and sad when we don't.

Some species, including humans, have taken that emotional processing a step further. We feel your emotions as well as ours, and we try to predict how you might behave and how that should affect the way we behave. When we mix together our basic emotions and yours, we create all manner of more complex emotions.

When we predict that you will cheat but you don't, we are surprised and happy. When we predict that you will cheat and you do, we are annoyed or angry. If we predict you will cooperate and you do, we feel trust or charity towards you. But if we predict you will cooperate and you don't, we feel alarm, vengefulness and jealousy because you ended up with a bigger reward. If we predict you will cheat and you don't, we feel admiration and trust, perhaps even love. If we cheat and you don't, we feel shame and remorse, which will motivate us not to cheat next time. In short, using a complex palette of our basic emotions and your basic emotions, we try to harmonise your future behaviour with ours.

In real life, the possible combinations and outcomes are much larger than in the prisoner's dilemma. So too are the possible blends and proportions of the basic emotions. This is perhaps why, while psychologists are largely in agreement about what our basic emotions are, there are a vast array of theories about what our so-called higher emotions are, and how many there are.

We call this ability to absorb other people's emotions, empathy. But no matter how it feels to us or how we describe it, at a neural level we are just trying to create outcomes where we both get $2 – the outcome where we feel love, happiness and charity. We do that using a specialist type of spindle neuron first completely described almost a hundred years ago by Constantin von Economo, an Austrian psychiatrist and neurologist. This is known as a von Economo neuron.

Our ability to automatically take account of other people and moderate our behaviour accordingly is dependent on von Economo neurons. Humans are not the only species where von Economo neurons have been found, but it is not a large club. They have only been reliably detected in chimpanzees, bonobos (pygmy chimps), gorillas and orangutans. They are also likely to be present in rhesus and macaque monkeys, and some research suggests they may exist in prairie voles (a type of rodent), whales, some dolphin species, hippos and elephants.

The number and concentration of these neurons in humans is not even on the same scale as the other species that have them. Adult humans have at least five times as many von Economo neurons as an adult gorilla, who in turn has at least five times the number found in a chimp or bonobo. Humans are not born with a complete set of von Economo neurons. Just prior to 42 weeks gestation we have none. At 42 weeks, that number jumps quickly to about the level of an adult chimp. By four months we have about the same number as an adult gorilla. By eight months we have around twice as many as an adult human, and then that number then steadily declines until by the age of four, we have the same amount as an adult human.

Anyone who has ever had anything to do with a baby would readily agree they are pretty low on empathy. They aren't too worried about how you feel, as long as they are changed, fed and watered. These numbers also suggest that eight month olds are overflowing with empathy, making them extraordinarily trusting. They aren't playing Tit for Tat, they are playing 'always trust everybody'. They then steadily prune the empathy circuits back as they learn about the adult world around them, until they are playing Tit for Tat just like an adult. From a developmental perspective, the late addition of von Economo neurons suggests that the number present in human adults is a very new evolutionary addition, possibly having occurred as recently as 100,000 years ago.

Why would the hardware for empathy have evolved in humans? Teams that work together do better than groups that don't, and that will only happen if those team members can trust each other not to cheat for personal gain. If I can feel what you feel, I will not harm you if I can avoid it. Not because I am altruistic, but because it is in my interest to do so. We are both paying a dollar because we get $2 and, importantly, we know that if we don't, neither of us will get anything. The best way to bind me to you is to bind my outcome to yours, and the best way to do that is to make me feel what you feel.

What happens if you don't develop the von Economo circuitry? You fail to acquire empathy and trust. Your development remains frozen at human version 1.0: pre-social human. You are unable to play Tit for Tat because you cannot trust anyone. And rather like a six month old, you are focused solely on your own needs without regard for anyone else. In short, you are a psychopath.

3

Psychopathy

WHAT HAPPENS WHEN EMPATHY FAILS?

Over the course of six years, Lee Holloway, a brilliant pro-grammer behind much of the code that secures the internet today, went from being a sociable, nurturing father and co-worker to being a jerk who showed no signs of caring about his wife, children or workmates. What caused this dramatic change in personality? Lee was suffering from a form of dementia which destroys von Economo neurons. When we lose that hardware, we become less human.

In the early 2000s, spam emails were growing in prevalence. And much of that spam was wildly inappropriate for young eyes. Motivated by the desire to protect children – and anyone else who didn't want to receive multiple invitations to increase their penis size – anti-spam legislation started to appear in US states. The laws allowed people to register their email address with the state. If a company spammed an address on the register they would be fined up to $5000 per message. Email marketing companies desperately needed a way to check that the email addresses on their lists were not on the do-not-spam register. Enter Matthew Prince, recent graduate from the University of Chicago Law School, who also happened to have an undergraduate degree in computer science.

Matthew had been working on an idea that would allow marketing companies to automatically check every email address against the registries. When he ran into computer science professor Arthur Keller at a conference in 2002, the idea became reality. Keller had been supervising a student project designed to do exactly the same thing. Keller and Prince shared the patent and started Unspam Technologies Inc. Employee number one was one of the students working on Keller's project: Lee Holloway.

Lee was an incredibly talented programmer capable of turning ideas into reality at unbelievable speed. Working for room and board, Lee produced technology that would lay the foundation for Cloudflare, one of the biggest cybersecurity firms on the planet today. About one fifth of all internet traffic is now routed through Cloudflare servers, which weed out spam and other threats before they get to their destination.

Besides being a gifted programmer, Lee was described by friends and co-workers alike as easygoing and fun to be around. In 2008, Lee married his college girlfriend, Alexandra. In late 2009, Lee and Matthew, together with a third founder, Michelle, decided to form Cloudflare. The company grew rapidly, and Lee was working long hours. But he mostly did this from home, so he could spend more time with Alexandra and their infant son.

He was a busy but playful and loving partner and dad. Until he wasn't.

By 2011 Alexandra noticed Lee had changed. He avoided playing with his son and wouldn't help around the house at all. He refused to go to parties and weddings with friends they'd known for years. He would look at meals Alexandra had cooked for him and then order pizza for himself instead. In short, he had become a jerk. In 2012, Alexandra decided to take an internship at NASA, which required her to move. When she told Lee she planned to take their son with her, he impassively asked her to get a divorce before she left.

At work, Lee was still a technical superstar, so while Prince thought his behaviour was strange, and he was surprised by the divorce, he put it down to the couple growing apart. Besides, it was really none of his business. Within months Lee had started dating Kristin, who ran communications at Cloudflare, and within a few years they were married.

Lee's behaviour at work had been gradually changing since Alexandra left. He was quick to anger, easily bored, and instead of helping and mentoring others, would angrily attack them if they made mistakes. By mid-2015, Lee's co-founders formally put him on an official performance improvement plan. By 2016, Lee's behaviour had become so destructive, they decided he needed to leave Cloudflare. Lee took the news in the same matter of fact way he'd taken the news that Alexandra was leaving.

Shortly afterwards, Kristin gave birth to their son. Lee was at the birth, but was completely disengaged other than to argue with the doctors about whether Kristin should have an epidural.

She didn't want one, and her doctors didn't want to administer one against her will, but Lee was insistent.

Once they were settled into married life, Lee started acting the way Alexandra had described. He was ordering takeaway instead of eating the meals Kristin prepared, and he spent most of his days sleeping or repeatedly watching *Home Alone*, an obsession he had recently acquired. Kristin couldn't get Lee to engage with their son at all. Whenever she pointed out that his behaviour was odd, he would simply concede it was, and promise to do better. But nothing changed.

Kristin eventually cajoled Lee into couples therapy, but he just sat through the sessions with a blank look on his face. In an interview with *Wired* magazine, Kristin recalled telling the therapist how Lee didn't seem to have any feelings for their son, nor any desire to interact with him. Rather than comfort or reassure Kristin, Lee stood up and announced he'd forgotten to return the bathroom key to the receptionist. He promptly left, and resumed sitting impassively when he returned. He gave no sign that he cared at all about what Kristin was saying.

Kristin initially put Lee's behaviour down to various life stresses, but a visit from her mother helped her see that this was more than transient stress or Lee just being a jerk. Kristin tried for months to get Lee to see medical professionals. Eventually she persuaded him to see a neurologist in the hope that an MRI might provide some answers. It did.

The MRI showed Lee had bvFTD, the behavioural variant of frontotemporal dementia, also known as Pick's disease. Pick's disease is the most common form of dementia in people under 60, and the third most common in people over 65. It is quite distinct from Alzheimer's disease, which has widespread effects on cognitive capabilities and memory. For people with Pick's disease, the damage is focused on the von Economo neurons. When scientists have analysed the brains of deceased sufferers, they have found that around 70 per cent of their von Economo neurons have been destroyed. A person with Pick's has intact cognitive powers and memory, but they are losing the ability to care about others. Their social wiring is eaten away, and their empathy, social awareness and self-control is seriously compromised.

People with Pick's disease lose the ability to judge socially appropriate behaviour. In one case, a patient's wife severed her finger while using borrowed gardening shears. She asked her husband to get her to the hospital. He agreed that she needed to go immediately, but insisted the gardening shears be returned to their neighbour first.

It is also common for Pick's disease sufferers to lose any sense of shame or embarrassment. Examples from published case studies include behaviours such as urinating in public, swimming nude in public pools, making inappropriate sexual advances, shoplifting, gambling, heavy drinking or digging through bins looking for food. They will often seek out confrontation, make hurtful or insensitive remarks to others, and even occasionally physically assault them. Their friends and family often describe them as being cold and unempathetic and showing no concern about the effects their behaviours have on others. The patient usually denies there is anything wrong at all.

Pick's disease sufferer Howard Glick is different. Glick has documented the course of his disease through video blogs and a documentary. He has also been instrumental in forming a signifi-cant online support group for sufferers. Early in the course of his disease, Glick told *Forbes* magazine that he felt 'psychologically intact' but felt that his filter was going. He can be inappropri-ately candid and frequently says things to strangers that get him in trouble. Howard says social interaction with people he is close to is also getting harder, because he just doesn't care – or, more accurately, it doesn't occur to him to care – how other people are. He says he can talk endlessly about himself but he has to remind himself to ask about others and try hard to be interested in their answers. This is distressing for him because he remembers what it was like to care and wants to regain that feeling. Glick says he wants to 'stay in the human race as long as possible'.

Pick's disease causes a change in personality. It initially attacks the von Economo neurons that give us the wiring for empathy, converting kind people into uncaring unempathetic jerks who struggle to participate in society. As it progresses, the degradation spreads to the temporal lobes of the brain, ultimately affecting the ability to use language. More and more of the brain is gradually affected until the symptoms start to look more like Alzheimer's disease, with the patient needing assistance with daily living and their memory being affected.

It took six years of unpleasant changes in Lee Holloway before his second wife managed to get him properly diagnosed. Because Pick's disease initially looks like the person is just behaving badly, it often takes this long before loved ones push a sufferer to seek medical help. And even if they approach doctors earlier, it is often misdiagnosed as a personality disorder or depression. According to his documentary, Howard Glick was given hundreds of different medications for mental illness, all of which did nothing, before a PET scan of his brain finally revealed his true diagnosis.

Are people like Lee Holloway or Howard Glick psychopaths? No, they are not. The first stages of Pick's disease look a lot like psychopathy, a behavioural disorder that has been recognised by psychiatry since its inception. But this doesn't mean a Pick's disease sufferer is a psychopath, it just gives us insight into the source of the problem: psychopaths have too few von Economo neurons.

1

In 1835, British physician James Prichard coined the term 'moral insanity'. At the time, 'moral' had a meaning closer to 'emotional' than 'ethical', so what Prichard meant was that the person was emotionally insane. Prichard used this term to describe people who suffered a 'perversion of feelings, affections and habits without any defect of reasoning faculties or hallucinations'. In other words, patients were prone to mania but were otherwise normal.

Half a century later, German doctor Julius Koch published his *Short Textbook of Psychiatry*, which included a similar condition in a group of chronic mental illnesses labelled 'psychopathic inferiority'.

The term 'psychopath' caught on and gained traction in the first decades of the twentieth century, but it was a very broad term. It was used to describe a range of behaviours deemed antisocial and perverse – which at the time included homosexuality – in people who otherwise were able to function normally in society.

It wasn't until American psychiatrist Hervey Cleckley published *The Mask of Sanity* in 1941 that the medical profession had a definitive description and diagnostic checklist of symptoms for what we would today describe as psychopathy.

Cleckley was an American psychiatrist who, after studying in Oxford on a Rhodes Scholarship, obtained his medical qualifications at the University of Georgia in 1929. He then went to work treating WWI veterans at the US Veterans Hospital No. 62, a large psychiatric hospital in Augusta, Georgia. In 1937, he became a professor of psychiatry at his old university. After taking up full-time teaching, he noticed the prevalence of a personality type in the community which he had seen a lot while working at the veterans' hospital. He dubbed this type of person a psychopath, and in *The Mask of Sanity* he set about documenting exactly what that meant.

Cleckley described a psychopath as being a person who appears normal but secretly engages in socially destructive behaviour. His book was intended to assist in detecting, diagnosing and managing this type of person. Based on his experience with veterans, he didn't believe the condition was curable. The purpose of the book was to help fellow professionals identify psychopaths and control the harm they could do to themselves and those around them.

Using a series of fifteen case studies, Cleckley created a list of sixteen behaviours which identify a psychopath. These included superficial charm, insincerity, lack of remorse, antisocial behaviour, failure to learn from experience, pathological egocentricity, poverty of emotional response, impersonal sex life and a lack of insight into their own condition. He also included some criteria to distinguish psychopathy from other disorders, such as lack of delusions or neuroses, and threats of suicide which are not carried out.

To Cleckley, the critical feature of psychopathy was what he called 'The Mask'. Psychopaths are superficially charming, socially poised and seemingly intelligent on the outside, but emotionally impoverished to a profound degree on the inside. He said the condition is marked by serious impulse control deficiencies. Cleckley observed that psychopaths frequently indulge in pointless antisocial behaviour which most people cannot understand. He said this was the underlying insanity that the mask concealed.

Cleckley also theorised that psychopaths suffer from a condition he described as 'semantic aphasia', meaning that psychopaths use the same words as everybody else – for example, 'I love you' – but are disconnected from the emotions that normally accompany them. As later researchers put it, they 'know the words but not the music'. He used Scarlett O'Hara as an example of what he meant.

Scarlett was the main character in the 1936 bestselling book *Gone with the Wind*. Scarlett's primary concern throughout the novel is her own wellbeing and happiness, even at the expense of those around her. She frequently ignores the feelings and needs of her family members, husband and friends, and has a habit of using people for her personal gain and then discarding them when they are no longer useful. An example is Scarlett's relentless pursuit of her wealthy neighbour Ashley Wilkes, despite being married herself and knowing that her actions would devastate his wife Melanie, who is also her close friend and sister-in-law.

While Cleckley was writing *The Mask of Sanity*, *Gone with the Wind* was released as a film, with Vivien Leigh playing Scarlett.

Cleckley described Scarlett as a 'partial-psychopath' who the author, Margaret Mitchell, had crafted very convincingly. He said Scarlett's incapacity for true love is unmodifiable and her 'ego-centricity is all but absolute'. Mitchell was flattered by the praise. She said she was bewildered and amused that the nation could applaud and take to its heart a 'frigid woman who loved attention and admiration for their own sake but had no comprehension of actual deep feelings and no reactions to the attentions of others'.

The Mask of Sanity was published just before the attack on Pearl Harbor forced the US to enter the Second World War, and Cleckley was anxious to ensure those responsible for military recruitment were aware of the potential problem. In an article published in the *Georgia Medical Journal* in 1941, he warned that medical examiners needed to be aware of the disorder. Cleckley said that the 'general medical man' would easily spot and exclude potential recruits suffering from delusions or hysteria, as well as psychotics and schizophrenics, but would not easily detect a psychopath. He explained that they would be impressive candidates. They would be eloquent, intelligent, often appear well educated and would be unlikely to show any of the classic symptoms of mental instability. He said they would display 'a perfect mask of genuine sanity, a flawless surface indicative in every respect of robust mental health'. Cleckley wrote that detecting them required taking a complete history and verifying as much of it as possible. That would likely reveal a chequered work history with frequent job changes, sometimes minor encounters with the law, and difficulties in maintaining relationships with friends and partners.

He cautioned it was important to identify psychopaths, warning that if admitted to the military they would prove to be a 'seriously disorganising influence'. They would fail regularly and blame their companions. Because of their superficial charm, they would create doubt and confusion while spreading dissatisfaction. If the psychopath is removed from the service, Cleckley warned, he will demand pensions and privileges for the rest of his life, claiming that the military caused his disability. He pointed out that it was generally accepted that on top of the effect on their fighting capability, each person with a personality disorder who was admitted to service would cost the military an estimated $30,000 (equivalent to $600,000 today) in ongoing compensation.

The Mask of Sanity was an instant and unexpected hit. There was something about the notion of mentally disordered people living in disguise among ordinary folk that caught the attention of the American public. The book was so popular that when the fledgling American Psychiatric Association produced its first diagnostic manual of mental disorders, commonly referred to as DSM I, in 1952, it adopted much of Cleckley's description. The personality disorder outlined by Cleckley appeared in the DSM as a 'sociopathic personality disturbance', and the authors made clear that the term included people previously described as psychopaths. The terms 'sociopath' and 'psychopath' were used interchangeably by doctors at the time, but there was an increasing tendency to use the word sociopath to avoid confusion between psychopaths and psychotics. Psychotics suffer from hallucinations and paranoia, and there is no real-world overlap between the disorders. According to the DSM, sociopaths were 'chronically antisocial' people who failed to learn from experience or punishment. They were pleasure seeking and callous, and had no sense of loyalty or responsibility to others.

By 1968, when the second edition of the DSM was released, a few more of Cleckley's criteria had been added to the diagnosis. The new 'antisocial personality disorder' description advised that patients would be 'grossly selfish, callous, irresponsible, impulsive, and unable to feel guilt or to learn from experience and punishment'. They would also be easily frustrated and have a tendency to blame others for their problems.

The difficulty with these descriptions was that it was almost impossible to get two psychologists or psychiatrists to agree on a diagnosis. A major study of diagnostic consistency released in 1974 found that agreement between professionals was little more than random chance. There was a good reason for this: they were being asked to match their impressions of a person to a narrative case study based on what they had observed during whatever time they had with the patient. This lack of consistency in diagnosis, coupled with the promotion of newly available drug therapies by manufacturers who attributed mental illness to chemical imbalances, created a demand for precise lists of symptoms that could potentially be addressed with pharmaceutical interventions.

The third edition of the DSM, released in 1980, was a major step backwards in our ability to identify and diagnose psychopaths. It almost entirely abandoned Cleckley's descriptions. The new antisocial personality disorder (ASPD) was based on nine very precisely defined symptoms including aggressiveness, poor work history, being an irresponsible parent, unlawful behaviour, infidelity, financial irresponsibility, recklessness and dishonesty. And each of these had very specific requirements. Recklessness, for example, required 'driving while intoxicated or recurrent speeding', and infidelity required 'two or more divorces or separations' or 'ten or more sexual partners' in a year. Now doctors could reliably diagnose ASPD just by using a checklist. Unfortunately, what they were diagnosing was not psychopathy.

Critical parts of Cleckley's definition had been dropped. The lack of remorse and shame, the inability to accept blame, the inability to learn from experience, egocentricity, inadequate depth of feeling and a lack of insight were all deleted as diagnostic criteria. In other words, the very things that demonstrated a lack of empathy, the core feature of psychopathy, were no longer in the diagnostic criteria. What was left was a shell of unpleasant behaviour that could have described anyone with antisocial tendencies and was only vaguely connected to psychopathy. Without clear guidance from the profession, and with the public drawing a link between the terms psychosis and psychopathy, the term 'psychopath' slid from diagnosis to defamatory insult. In the public mind, a psychopath was no longer a person suffering from a lack of empathy. Instead, they were a malevolent, evil, probable killer. It's little wonder HR will have a hard time pinning the label of 'psychopath' on someone.

Using these criteria, it was entirely possible to be diagnosed as a 'psychopath' and not actually be one, and equally if not more likely to actually be a psychopath and remain undiagnosed. With the release of DSM III in 1980, we no longer had an official diagnosis for psychopathy or sociopathy. Instead, we were left with a pointless diagnosis of antisocial-ness. While psychopaths can be antisocial, the vast majority of people who would be diagnosed as antisocial using the DSM III would not be psychopaths.

The profession recognised that perhaps they had sacrificed validity for reliability, and in 1987 released an update, the DSM III-R, which added lack of remorse and impulsivity back into the definition of antisocial personality disorder. Once again, very specific requirements were laid out. Impulsivity required 'travelling from place to place without a pre-arranged job' or 'lack of a fixed address'. It was a small improvement, but still a long way short of Cleckley's definition.

The 1994 release, DSM IV, didn't change the definition much. There had been a move within the profession to reinstate lack of empathy, glib charm and arrogance, but these were also part of the newly created condition of 'narcissistic personality disorder'. It was decided it would be confusing to have such a high degree of overlap between two conditions that the profession had decided were entirely separate. As a result, those vital characteristics of psychopathy were not reinstated as part of the definition of ASPD. Narcissistic personality disorder is characterised by a pattern of grandiosity, a constant need for admiration and a lack of empathy for others. Both disorders involve difficulties in understanding the needs of others, but the core difference lies in the underlying motivations. Antisocial personality disorder involves a high degree of impulsivity and often criminal behaviour, whereas narcissistic personality disorder is marked by a need for the approval of others and grandiosity. Needless to say, even without adding 'lack of empathy' back into the definition of antisocial personality disorder, there is still a large overlap in presentation, and it is not unusual for people to be diagnosed with both disorders.

The fifth and latest version of the DSM was released in 2013. Its contribution was to add social assertiveness, emotional resilience and fearlessness, collectively referred to as 'boldness', as a requirement in what it called the 'psychopathy specifier' to a diagnosis of antisocial personality disorder. Cleckley did suggest that psychopaths lack anxiety in situations that would make the rest of us cautious, but he did not consider it important enough to include it in his list of diagnostic criteria, other than to say psychopaths don't learn from failure.

Critically, DSM 5 did nothing to address the gaping hole at the centre of its recommendations. Yet again, the profession had ignored the primary differentiating feature of psychopathy: the lack of empathy. The current definition of antisocial personality disorder does not require that the patient lacks empathy.

In 1941, Cleckley provided the psychiatric profession with an elegant and accurate description of psychopathy. His definition was adopted for the first 40 years of the diagnostic manual. But since 1980, the profession has doggedly retreated from that definition, to the point where it is now impossible to accurately diagnose someone with one of the most common and most dangerous mental health conditions.

Cleckley described a personality type which he encountered daily in the community. His description closely matched a type that had been documented for as long as the psychiatric profession had existed, and remains to this date the most accurate description of a person whose empathy circuitry has failed or was never there in the first place. There is still no official diagnosis of psychopathy available to the psychiatric profession, but we would be foolish to assume that means they don't exist.

Given the failure of the psychiatric profession to come up with a diagnosis, is there a way to reliably diagnose psychopaths? Thankfully, yes, but there are problems; we are hard-wired to trust other humans, but diagnosis requires subjective assessments of a personality type that has deception as one of its defining features.

2

Frustrated by his profession's retreat from a diagnosis that could be used on the patients he saw every day, prison psychologist Robert Hare created a usable tool which has set the standard for practical detection of psychopaths. Necessity is the mother of invention, and nowhere is there a greater need to accurately detect psychopaths than in prisons.

In 1960, Hare had just finished his Master's degree and needed a job. He took the first one he could get, working as a psychologist in a maximum-security prison on the outskirts of Vancouver, Canada. His job was to assess the psychological health of prisoners, but he had no experience as a practising psychologist or of working in prisons, and quickly found himself being manipulated by some of the inmates. He found that the guards knew more about the prisoners than any of the available tests could tell him. After a rough eight months, he was relieved to escape back to academia and work on his doctorate, focusing on the behavioural effect of reward and punishment.

It wasn't long before Hare came upon Cleckley's *The Mask of Sanity*, full of case studies from the veterans' hospital. Hare immediately recognised the personality type Cleckley was describing. He had encountered prisoners who were smooth talking and charming on the surface but lacked empathy, remorse and impulse control, had no regard for social rules and callously exploited others to get what they wanted. Having worked with them at close quarters and felt their menace, Hare was fascinated by the concept of psychopathy, and it became his professional focus from then on. By 1963 he had completed his doctorate and taken up a professorship at the University of British Columbia in Vancouver. Picking up on the concept of fearlessness, or lack of anxiety, mentioned by Cleckley, Hare set up experiments aimed at determining if psychopaths responded differently to punishment.

In one of his first trials, Hare arranged for eleven psychopathic criminals, eleven non-psychopathic criminals and eleven community controls to be hooked up to a device that they were told would give them a short but strong electric shock after an eight-second countdown. Skin conductance monitors recorded the level of anticipatory stress each person was experiencing by measuring the amount of sweat on their skin as they waited for the shock. Unsurprisingly, Hare found that the non-psychopaths became significantly stressed as the count approached eight seconds. The psychopaths, however, were experiencing much less stress.

Hare followed that experiment with a similar trial designed to tease out humans' preference for delayed or immediate punishment.

In that trial, Hare asked twelve psychopathic criminals, twelve non-psychopathic criminals and nineteen community controls to either receive an immediate shock or one delayed by ten seconds. Over 80 per cent of the non-psychopaths chose to be shocked immediately, but only about half of the psychopaths did. Normal people would rather get it over with. They would rather not have to sit there for ten seconds anticipating the pain. The psychopaths were quite happy to wait.

From this series of experiments, Hare theorised that, as Cleckley had suggested, psychopaths are less anxious in the face of punishment and therefore much harder to threaten or punish. Potential prison time or any other punishment is much less of a deterrent to a psychopath than to the rest of us. That, combined with their ability to charm parole boards, is likely to explain why the average psychopath will be imprisoned and released three times before the average non-psychopath with the same sentence is back once.

Hare was practically the only person studying psychopaths in the 1960s, but he persisted. He had been using the DSM descriptions to determine the level of psychopathy in the subjects of his trials, but he found their imprecise narrative and case study-based format hard to apply. By the mid-1970s he had decided he needed a more precise tool. He started with simple checklists based on Cleckley's sixteen criteria, but he needed a scoring system to enable consistent comparison.

By 1980, the year any semblance of psychopathy was effectively removed from the DSM, he was ready to publish his tool, the 22-item Psychopathy Checklist (PCL). Much to Hare's frustration, the rest of his profession had effectively deleted the condition of psychopathy. He knew that not only was it very real, it affected large numbers of people. He knew the world needed an accurate diagnostic tool, and that the worst thing we could do would be to pretend the condition didn't exist at all. In 1991, Hare released a revised version, the PCL-R, which had been trimmed back to twenty items. It was designed in such a way that any researcher could reliably and consistently use it. It quickly became the gold standard in measuring psychopathy, despite there being no official diagnosis.

The checklist runs through the Cleckley criteria, such as superficial charm, egocentricity, pathological lying, lack of emotional response, remorse and empathy, impulsivity, failure to accept responsibility and promiscuous sexual behaviour, but adds in some other criteria that reflect the tool's development for use in criminal populations. Those are items such as parasitic lifestyle, juvenile delinquency, criminal versatility, early behaviour problems and previous revocation of parole.

Researchers are asked to measure each item on a three-point scale. Zero means the criteria does not apply at all, one is for a partial match and two is for a good match. The score is then totalled to give a psychopathy score with a maximum of 40. Researchers generally use 25 or more as the cut-off for psychopathy. Most people would rate around four or five. If your only symptom is being an egomaniac who loves posting selfies, then you will come away with a two on egocentricity, but still fall well short of being a psychopath. To get up to clinical levels of concern, you'd need to be more like James Bond.

CASE STUDY: JAMES BOND

PCL-R	James Bond
Facet 1: Interpersonal	
Glibness or superficial charm	2 – Is it possible to be more charming than James Bond?
Grandiose sense of self-worth	2 – A 'secret' agent who uses his own name all the time? – yup.
Pathological lying	2 – Other than about his name, he does seem to lie an awful lot.
Cunning or manipulative	2 – Obviously part of the job.
Facet 2: Affective	
Lack of remorse or guilt	2 – Bond has killed over 350 people on screen so far and it never seems to trouble him in the slightest.
Emotionally shallow	2 – I'm sure he really does love all those women he sleeps with.
Callous or lack of empathy	2 – Has he ever seemed to experience another person's emotions? Okay, there was that one time when he cried in the shower with Vesper Lynd . . .
Failure to accept responsibility for their own actions	1 – Every now and then he does take the blame for stuffing up.
Facet 3: Lifestyle	
Need for stimulation (easily bored)	2 – We never see him sitting around much, do we?
Parasitic lifestyle	2 – Everything seems to be on the expense account.

Lack of realistic, long-term goals	2 – Does he have any long-term goals?
Impulsivity	2 – He certainly struggles to contain his impulses when it comes to killing and seducing women.
Irresponsibility	1 – Occasionally he does things for king and country.

Facet 4: Antisocial

Poor behavioural controls	0 – He is in control most of the time.
Early behavioural problems	0 – We don't know, so let's go with 0.
Juvenile delinquency	0 – Once again, we don't know.
A history of having conditional release from prison revoked	0 – We don't know.
Criminal versatility	0 – His crimes are sanctioned by his 00 status.

Other Items

Many short-term marital relationships	1 – He's never been married, but he has had many relationships that might have ended that way, had the other half not been killed off.
Promiscuous sexual behaviour	2 – Is it possible to give more than 2?
Total	27

The PCL methodology has proven itself to be a reliable and consistent measure of psychopathy. It is, without doubt, a significantly more useful tool than the DSM, but it does have some drawbacks. A proper assessment can only be performed after a two-hour interview with the person, and requires access to independent records about their upbringing and criminal history. That's why, for example, I couldn't score James Bond at all on five of the twenty criteria. And because it was developed for use with criminals, it's probable that its results are skewed to unsuccessful psychopaths – that is, those that get caught. Because of these limitations, researchers have developed a number of tools designed for use in non-criminal populations. Like the PCL, they are based on Cleckley's descriptions, but they reduce or remove the reliance on criminal history. One of the most popular is the Psychopathic Personality Inventory (PPI), created by US psychologist Scott Lilienfeld and first released in 1996.

The PPI asks us to rate ourselves on a four-point scale (false, mostly false, mostly true, true) when presented with a series of statements like 'Most people would describe me as charming and nonchalant – I can turn my charm on and off like a faucet.' Our answers are then used to create a score that measures our levels of empathy, charm, remorse, impulsivity, fearlessness, tendency to blame others, regard for social norms and stress immunity.

Researchers using the PPI no longer need access to your criminal history or to sit you down for an extended interview. They can simply ask you to fill in a questionnaire, or even ask someone who knows you well to answer it on your behalf. Oxford University psychologist Kevin Dutton did exactly that when he asked experienced political reporters and biographers to complete a PPI assessment of the 2016 US presidential candidates, as well as of some famous historical figures. Dutton says it is revealing to see who scores in the top 20 per cent.

Unlike Hare's PCL, the PPI does not have a cut-off score that allows you to declare someone a psychopath. Rather, it is presented as a continuum. Saddam Hussein scored the highest of the men who were studied, with Henry the Eighth coming in second and Idi Amin close behind. Then came Donald Trump, followed by Adolf Hitler, William the Conqueror and Ted Cruz. Hillary Clinton lagged a little further behind but still scored unusually highly, given that women normally score lower on PPI tests.

Perhaps a little more surprisingly, Saint Paul, Jesus and Winston Churchill all had scores similar to Ted Cruz. The PPI provides scores on eight facets, and these people tended to score high on blaming others and rebellious non-conformity. If, however, we zero in on just the traits that must be there if a person lacks von Economo neurons – lack of empathy and callousness – we get a slightly different leader board. The top few change their order a bit, but it's still pretty much the same crew. Adolf Hitler now comes in first, followed by Saddam Hussein, Idi Amin and Donald Trump, with Ted Cruz and Henry the Eighth tied for fifth place. Hillary Clinton jumps into sixth spot, just ahead of Napoleon. But Jesus now drops to the bottom of the list, behind Mahatma Gandhi and Abraham Lincoln.

Unlike the DSM, both the PCL and the PPI are based on Cleckley's diagnostic criteria, but they have their weaknesses. The PCL is the gold standard when it comes to criminal psychopaths, but it is heavily reliant on the subject having a history of inter-action with the justice system. The PPI can be used on more diverse populations and without access to a criminal history, but is dependent on honest responses from a population who have dis-honesty as a defining characteristic. If it is applied to public figures it can confuse characteristics of good leadership, such as rebellious non-conformity, with psychopathic features. There is a world of difference between Jesus and Saint Paul refusing to conform with Roman rule and a psychopath subverting social norms.

Is there a more definitive way to diagnose a psychopath? Yes, but it requires some serious diagnostic equipment. Unfortunately, in order to determine von Economo neuron density, the patient needs to be dead so we can put slices of their brain under a micro-scope. While that is highly accurate, it is unlikely to take off as a diagnostic technique. Within the last fifteen years, however, advances in medical technology have delivered a method that is almost as reliable: the functional MRI.

3

One of Hare's students at the University of British Colombia was Kent Kiehl, who worked on his Master's degree and doc-torate under Hare during the 1990s. Kiehl grew up in Tacoma, Washington, in the same neighbourhood as Ted Bundy.

Theodore 'Ted' Bundy was perhaps America's most famous serial killer. Just before his execution in 1989 he confessed to killing 30 women between 1974 and 1978, having spent the previous decade denying he had killed any. Investigators believe the toll was much higher than the 30 he admitted to. Bundy was intelligent, charismatic and good-looking. He used his attractiveness to approach victims in public and lure them to secluded locations where he raped and eventually killed them. He would often revisit crime scenes and perform sexual acts long after their death. He also hacked off at least twelve of his victims' heads and kept them as souvenirs.

Bundy was arrested in 1975 but escaped several times before being arrested again in 1978 and sentenced to death in 1980. He was the subject of many psychiatric examinations during his nine-year stint on death row, and it seemed as if the diagnoses were as varied as the people making them. Manic depression, multiple personality disorder and narcissistic personality disorder all registered as potential explanations, but the consensus was that antisocial personality disorder was the best match. There was also a strong consensus that Bundy was perfectly sane, not suffering any kind of psychosis and knew exactly what he was doing. He frequently told FBI interviewers and doctors that he felt no guilt or remorse and accepted no responsibility. He was also universally acknowledged by all his interviewers as being highly manipulative.

Kiehl says he was partly driven to study psychopathy by the incongruence between Bundy's charming veneer of normality and the horrific crimes he committed. He wanted to understand what made someone like that tick. After Hare closed his department at the University of British Colombia in 2000, Kiehl went on to do postgraduate work at Yale before being recruited by the Mind Research Network (MRN), a non-profit working with the University of New Mexico. His work was focused on establishing whether psychopathy could be diagnosed using brain imaging technology.

Kiehl's research is extraordinarily comprehensive. He has travelled throughout various US prison systems with the MRN's mobile MRI scanner built into a truck. The scanner has enabled him to perform examinations in numbers that were previously impossible. Transporting a prisoner to an MRI scanner in a hospital is a task fraught with risk of escape and complicated by elaborate security measures and significant cost. Before he had access to the mobile scanner, Kiehl had done some MRI-based studies in prison, but it was not possible to work with the kinds of numbers needed for robust research. He was scanning eight people when he needed to scan 800. Kiehl's mobile scanner enabled him to image the brains of over 5000 prisoners while they performed tasks designed to stimulate empathetic reactions.

Before imaging commences, Kiehl has full psychopathic evaluations done based on Hare's PCL testing regime for prisoners. Once the results are in, he creates groupings of psychopaths and non-psychopaths that are matched on IQ, educational background and the type of crime committed. Then each prisoner is placed, one at a time, in the MRI scanner to complete a word-based task, followed by a similar task based on images. Kiehl keeps the tasks simple to reduce the potential for psychopaths to try and manipulate the results.

First, the inmate is shown a series of words and phrases and asked to rate each one as being morally offensive or not. A phrase like 'sex with your mother' is intended to be offensive, while 'listening to others' is not. Some ambiguous words like 'abortion' are also part of the list. Then the same task is done with images. Perhaps a photo of a baby covered in blood is shown, but it is clear the child has just been born. Then an image of a man whose head has been beaten in with a club is shown. Each time, the subject has to say whether the phrase or the image is morally offensive. The researchers record the prisoners' answers and the speed with which they give them, and the scanner simultaneously monitors blood flow to various parts of their brain, an indicator of brain activity. The scans are then compared with those from the matched non-psychopathic criminals, as well as a control group of people from the community who have never been convicted of a crime.

Using the functional MRI technology, Kiehl has been able to show that when processing moral questions, psychopaths show less coordinated activity between the amygdala, where we process our basic emotions – fear, aggression, happiness and sadness – and the anterior prefrontal cortex, the most recently evolved part of our brain, responsible for processing higher emotions and moderating social behaviour.

The anterior prefrontal cortex is roughly twice the size, relatively speaking, of the same area in bonobo chimpanzees, our closest living relative. It is involved in complex planning and reasoning. This is not a part of the brain that instinctively reacts like the amygdala, it is the bit that allows us to keep multiple goals in mind simultaneously, and to run simulations of other possible scenarios. This is the impulse controller, the strategic planner and the considered decision-maker. Kiehl found that connections to this area were disrupted in psychopaths and confirmed other research which showed that in psychopaths, this part of the brain was up to 17 per cent smaller than in non-psychopaths. This might go a long way towards explaining their lack of impulse control and how poorly psychopaths do when they sniff a reward. In the psychopath, the primitive reward-seeking amygdala overrides the more considered risk assessment of the prefrontal cortex.

4

Long before the invention of MRI machines, researchers had a pretty reliable tool for measuring dysfunction in the frontal lobes of the brain: a pack of cards. Since 1948, psychologists have been diagnosing acquired brain injury using a test which requires the participant to sort a deck of specially designed cards.

The Wisconsin Card Sorting Test verifies an individual's competence in abstract reasoning and their ability to change

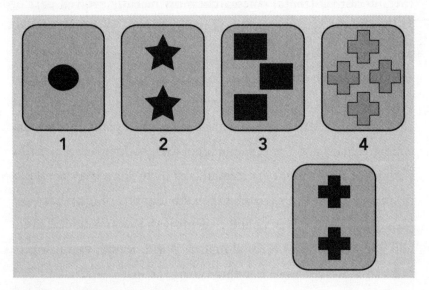

The Wisconsin Card Sorting Test

problem-solving strategies when the situation changes. The test can be scored using a well-defined set of quantitative measures, and is regarded as being highly reliable.

In this test, you are shown cards one by one. You are told to place the card you are given on the pile that matches best, but you are not told what the rule for matching is. In the pictured example, the secret rule might be to match colours, so if you put the card with two red crosses on pile 1, a card with one red circle, you would be correct; or it could be to match the number of shapes, in which case putting it on pile 2 would be correct; or it might be to match the shape, so putting it on pile 4 would be correct.

If you start putting the cards in the right piles according to the secret rule, you get a monetary reward for each correct card. If you are wrong, you are fined. By trial and error, people quickly figure out how to sort the cards for maximum reward. Then, without telling you, the researchers change the rule. You only know the rule has changed because the rewards and punishments have changed. A card that previously would have earned a reward now suddenly gets a fine.

People with injury to the anterior prefrontal cortex and psychopaths are significantly less able to change their previously chosen strategy, even as the losses mount up. Non-psychopaths slow down after the matching strategy changes and their losses increase. They think about it more, and adjust their strategy to avoid further loss. But psychopaths speed up and chase the reward harder.

Psychopaths universally do much worse on this sort of study than non-psychopaths. But this is only true if the rewards and punishments are given out as the cards are dealt. If the subjects are just told a card placement is correct or incorrect and a tally is provided at the end, the psychopaths perform the same as the non-psychopaths. If the psychopath's desire for reward remains actively in play, they cannot easily change strategy. But if it is theoretical, they don't do any better or worse than the rest of us. The presence of palpable reward seems to produce an 'action stations' response in psychopaths. When they are in this state, they are hyper-alert and ready to respond quickly. They are also highly resistant to changing their planned response. Instant gratification has the same effect on psychopaths as alcohol has on the rest of us. It disables their inhibitions and makes them want to chase the reward harder.

More recently Kiehl has been using diffusion tensor images, a type of MRI scan which can map connections between parts of the brain. These have confirmed that the tissue containing von Economo neurons connecting the amygdala to the anterior prefrontal cortex, known as the temporal pole, is disrupted in psychopaths and that there is reduced responsivity in those circuits during emotional processing and moral decision-making. The temporal poles are also the parts of the brain which become damaged in patients with Pick's disease, the dementia that makes people behave like psychopaths.

The failure in those circuits does more than disrupt emotional and moral processing. It also interferes with our reward system. Unlike the rest of us, psychopaths do not learn from reward or punishment.

A long series of functional MRI studies show that the parts of the brain responsible for teaching us about risky and rewarding things are not engaged in psychopathic brains. The reward system is activated by dopamine, and makes us chase rewards and run from danger. Dopamine is our motivating neurotransmitter. It is not inherently rewarding, but its presence means we are either about to be rewarded or are in danger. In non-psychopaths, dopamine levels are a means of coding the level of reward or danger we experience, so we can make accurate predictions about whether to run towards or away from those things in future. We are initially driven to chase a reward or run from danger by the older, more primitive part of our brain: the amygdala. We then code how satisfying and worthwhile that decision was using the more recently evolved prefrontal cortex. These two regions communicate using von Economo neurons. If we don't have von Economo neurons, we cannot properly encode the dopamine signal for rewards and punishments.

Kiehl's decades-long research imaging the brains of criminal psychopaths provides confirmation that psychopathy is a hardware failure. Psychopaths have limited connection between their primal emotional core and the much more recently evolved executive control area in the brain. This impairs their capacity for empathy, impulse control and other higher order social functions. It also impairs their ability to accurately judge the value of a reward or punishment.

Psychopaths learn from neither rewards nor punishments. They do not moderate their desire for reward with an assessment of the risks. Equally, they have no regard for potential danger, because their brains did not properly encode the consequences of those actions the last time they performed them. When psychopaths perform the Wisconsin Card Sorting Test, they are less able to adjust strategy because they are simply not learning from their mistakes. The upside for a psychopath is that because they cannot learn, they have no anxiety about potential loss or punishment. They truly live in the moment. This is why the failure of your psychopathic boss's customer acquisition strategy will not deter her from using it again, and again, and again. Doubling down is a psychopath's solution to a failed plan. All the while, the team charged with re-implementing the failed strategy becomes more and more frustrated, and the business suffers greater and greater losses.

In human society, our ability to survive is dependent on our ability to cooperate, which is in turn based on our ability to trust one another. Trust saves time and effort and provides group-powered leverage. With trust, the whole truly is greater than the sum of each of our individual efforts. With trust, we are the 1980 Miracle on Ice; without it, we are the 2004 'Dream Team'. Without trust, we will fall victim to the tragedy of the commons, and we will all lose in the end. But in order to trust, we need to be wired for empathy. As Kiehl's research confirms, some of us just aren't.

Can psychopathy be cured? Unfortunately, the answer appears to be no. The best that can be said is that some of the worst criminal outcomes related to psychopathy can be constrained using what we know about the way psychopaths process rewards and punishment.

*

5

In the mid-1980s, an epidemic of youth violence fuelled by crack cocaine and cheap handguns engulfed the United States. By the early nineties, four out of every five violent crimes were being committed by people under the age of eighteen. Between 1988 and 1994 violent crime arrest rates for young people doubled. Prisons filled quickly and US lawmakers scrambled for solutions.

In Wisconsin, the legislature recognised that the current system was failing. The statistics showed that young offenders were being locked in juvenile prison until they were released as adults to commit more, and more violent, crimes. They decided to try something different. Established in 1995, the Mendota Juvenile Treatment Center is a 29-bed juvenile psychiatric facility aimed at breaking the cycle of criminal pathology. The idea was that the state's high-security juvenile prison would transfer its most mentally ill boys aged twelve to seventeen to Mendota for treatment. Mendota was operated by the Wisconsin Health Department, not the Department of Corrections, and it was run by psychologists Michael Caldwell and Greg Van Rybroek. The staff were medical workers, not prison guards. There was one staff member for every three kids – four times the ratio in a correction facility.

Caldwell and Van Rybroek were expecting to receive kids suffering classic mental illnesses such as psychosis or schizophrenia. What they got were psychopaths. The most menacing, callous and recalcitrant kids were flooding Mendota. All prisoners transferred to Mendota had been deemed uncontrollable at other institutions. None of the classic treatments worked, and neither did ramping up the punishment. Largely by trial and error, Caldwell and Van Rybroek developed a treatment at Mendota which seemed to constrain psychopathy, although it clearly didn't cure it. Their breakthrough involved working *with* the psychopathic brain, rather than against it. They designed a system that emphasised rewards and downplayed punishment – after all, if punishment worked with these kids, they wouldn't be in Mendota in the first place. What they found is that the kids responded enthusiastically to reward.

The Mendota reward system is rather like a frequent flyer program, but for good behaviour rather than flying. Prisoners are constantly monitored by all staff. Any sign of positive behaviour, no matter how small, is reinforced with a points reward. As those points accumulate, prisoners attain entry to increasingly more prestigious levels called Club 19, Club 23 and the VIP Club. Each increase in status earns them greater trust and privileges, such as chocolate bars, later bedtimes, Pokémon and baseball cards, pizza on Saturdays or more time on gaming devices. Bad behaviour costs points, but the punishment is short-lived and the points can be quickly earned back. As other researchers, including Kent Kiehl, would later prove, due to the wiring deficiencies in the psychopathic brain, punishment does not change a psychopath's behaviour, but reward does.

The Mendota reward-focused system does make psychopaths easier to manage while they are detained, but does it change outcomes once they are released? The answer is that there are promising results in the short term, and it is certainly more effective at lowering the rate of repeat offending than any other attempted treatment of psychopathic prisoners.

Dog owners are likely thinking the Mendota system sounds an awful lot like the way you train a puppy. This is actually a useful way to think of psychopaths. As far as we can determine, humans are among the few animals to have developed the von Economo circuitry for empathy, and domestic dogs definitely have not. This, of course, means that dogs have no empathy. They cannot feel how you feel, and they cannot automatically use your emotions in calculations about how they should behave. But just like psychopaths, they can and do observe us in micro-detail, and consciously act in ways that they know we want. This is because 10,000 years of co-evolution has created a dependency in domesticated dogs. They need humans for survival, and they have learned how to stay on our good side. Dogs respond to withdrawal of treats or attention. They work hard to please us, so long as we reward good behaviour. The Wisconsin Card Sorting Test tells us that, just as with dogs, the reward for psychopaths must be immediate and tangible.

Hitting a dog does not change its behaviour for the better. Dogs, like psychopaths, do not respond to physical pain or punishment – they just become aggressive, or learn to be more furtive in doing the things you don't like. Hit a puppy for peeing on the lounge and next time he'll pee behind the lounge, where you are less likely to notice. The behaviour doesn't change, but the sneakiness does. Hit an adult dog for peeing on the lounge and he might take your hand off in response.

No-one at Mendota believes that this system will cause the inmates to develop empathy or a moral conscience, but the hope is that they will learn a cognitive version of both that teaches them that life can be more rewarding if they play by the rules. Caldwell and Van Rybroek hope that the program gives inmates enough training to stay on the right side of the law. Studies of released Mendota prisoners do bear that out to an extent.

Two years after release, 40 per cent of the demographically matched psychopaths from a normal juvenile prison were back inside for violent crimes, but just 15 per cent of the psychopaths from Mendota had reoffended. After four years, 64 per cent of Mendota offenders had been rearrested, but that still compared favourably to 98 per cent of demographically matched inmates from other facilities. The Mendota system is not a cure or even a reliable constraint for psychopathic behaviour, but it is good evidence that systems of control that are focused on reinforcing desired behaviour are more likely to be effective than those focused on punishment.

Can empathy be taught? Yes, but only to a limited extent. Psychopaths lack the von Economo wiring necessary to experience true emotional empathy. But like dogs and the Mendota inmates, people can be trained to consciously pay attention to the things humans are likely to be feeling, and to react appropriately. Skilled leaders can control psychopaths by using a combination of rewards for preferred behaviour and non-negotiable transparency and honesty. In a workplace, this would look like leadership that is uncompromising on protecting the welfare of its employees, customers and suppliers and where profit is very much a secondary consideration. That kind of leadership forces a psychopath to do something they normally would not do – place the needs of others ahead of theirs. It can be done. A little later on we'll take a close look at Costco, a company that has achieved enormous success by doing just that.

6

At 8.46 on the morning of 11 September 2001, American Airlines Flight 11 from Boston to Los Angeles crashed into the North Tower of the World Trade Center in New York. Seventeen minutes later, American Airlines Flight 77 from Washington to Los Angeles, the second plane hijacked by Islamic jihadists, ploughed into the South Tower. Another plane was flown into the Pentagon, and a fourth aircraft crashed in an empty field in Pennsylvania after passengers swarmed the hijackers. In all, 2977 people were killed by the attacks that morning.

Hours after the planes hit, as airwaves were flooded with the vision of people falling from the towers, Donald Trump phoned in to local TV station WWOR to do an interview with his former publicist and friend Alan Marcus, who was appearing on air that day as a local analyst. Trump lived and worked in New York, and said he had seen the first impact on TV but then had watched the attack unfold from the windows of his home and office in Trump Tower. In the interview, Trump does not sound at all disturbed by what is unfolding in the city around him. He doesn't sound upset or angry, doesn't suggest retaliation or speculate as to who was responsible. His responses are matter of fact. In answer to Marcus's concern about 40 Wall Street, a 71-storey building owned by Trump near the Twin Towers, he says, 'Actually [that building] was the second-tallest building in downtown Manhattan, and it was actually, before the World Trade Center, was the tallest – and then, when they built the World Trade Center, it became known as the second-tallest. And now it's the tallest.' He goes on to express disappointment that the stock exchange had been closed because of the attack.

There were many things to think about that morning. Most of us who lived through it were experiencing, in real time, the incomprehensible shock of thousands of people just like us perishing in a city just like ours because of random acts of violence. But to Trump, the more important fact was that he now owned the tallest building in downtown New York. There didn't seem to be any emotional weight to the facts flying at him from the TV screen or through the windows of his apartment, and so the most important facts were the ones that directly affected him.

Sixteen years later, Trump was no longer a little-known New York real estate investor. He was President of the United States, on a flying visit to storm-devastated Puerto Rico. Two weeks earlier, the US territory had been smashed by the worst hurricane in its history. The island in the Caribbean was home to 3.4 million US citizens. The storm had completely destroyed the territory's power and communication systems. At the time of Trump's visit, more than 90 per cent of the population were still without power and the true extent of the devastation was still not certain. Trump's televised meeting with the Governor, Ricardo Rosselló, started well – and then went very bad, very quickly.

Referring to Katrina, the hurricane that had devastated New Orleans twelve years earlier, Trump said, 'Every death is a horror, but if you look at a real catastrophe like Katrina, and you look at the tremendous – hundreds and hundreds and hundreds of people that died, and you look at what happened here, with really a storm that was just totally overpowering, nobody's ever seen anything like this.' The President then noted that just sixteen people had reportedly been killed, and went on to complain that the storm recovery was costing the US a lot of money, saying, 'You've thrown our budget a little out of whack . . . but that's fine.'

Trump then toured the capital, San Juan, stopping in at a relief distribution point. Surrounded by a crowd of desperate people, Trump started throwing rolls of paper towel and other provisions into the crowd like he was Oprah tossing gifts to her audience. Footage of the incident went viral, with many saying it showed the President's total lack of empathy.

Trump was shocked by the reaction. He had helped distribute a high-quality product to people who needed it. He said, 'They had these beautiful, soft towels. Very good towels, and I came in and there was a crowd of a lot people. And they were screaming and they were loving everything. I was having fun. They were having fun. They said, "Throw 'em to me! Throw 'em to me, Mr. President."' He went on, 'So next day they said, "Oh it was so disrespectful to the people." It was just a made-up thing.' Trump did not understand why throwing relief provisions at survivors might offend people, and even after suffering a significant backlash still had no clue why people might be upset. Once again, he focused on irrelevant details like the quality of the towels. Once again, for Trump there was no emotional weight in what was happening. To him, there was no difference between throwing candy to kids at a Halloween party and distributing supplies to people whose lives had been destroyed.

Four months later, on 14 February 2018, nineteen-year-old Nikolas Cruz walked into the Marjory Stoneman Douglas High School in Florida armed with a semi-automatic rifle and started firing indiscriminately. He kept firing for six minutes before his weapon jammed. By then, fourteen students and three staff members were dead, and seventeen more people were critically injured.

One week later, Trump held a 'listening session' with the massacre survivors on how to combat gun violence in American schools. This time, his advisors were hoping to head off any empathy misfires. There were several photographers present, and some of them managed to get clear shots of Trump's short hand-written notes. The notes seemed to be a reminder to Trump that humans expect empathy in situations such as these. The first note was a prompt: 'What would you most want me to know about your experience?' The last note was a reminder to listen to people. The President apparently needed written notes to remind him that he should pay attention to the emotions of the survivors of the worst high-school massacre in US history, just a week after their friends, colleagues and children had been slaughtered in their classrooms.

Trump's notes were a reminder to engage in empathetic actions. That sort of intentional activation of empathy is what people who study this sort of thing call 'cognitive empathy'. For most of us, empathy is engaged automatically in response to experiencing the emotions of another person. If we were to speak to the mother of a child who'd been gunned down at school a week prior, we would have no choice in how we felt. We would feel her sorrow and pain as if it were our own child who had been killed. We would listen to her, console her and offer to help in any way we could. We would do the things Trump's notes reminded him to do. But we wouldn't need notes to remind us – we'd already be doing it.

Cognitive empathy is the real-world manifestation of the emotional empathy our von Economo neurons make us feel. But if you don't have von Economo neurons, you can't feel that empathy. You need notes to remind you how to act when people fly aeroplanes into buildings, hurricanes destroy people's lives and children are mown down by gunmen.

Not all psychopaths need notes. Dogs have spent millennia watching us closely and noticing what reactions to our expressions will get them fed. The inmates of Mendota who managed not to reoffend had learned to pay attention to the behaviour lessons taught by the psychologists running the facility. And intelligent psychopaths who have never been anywhere near a prison have been practising cognitive empathy since childhood. Knowing when to behave empathetically is critical to maintaining the mask of sanity. Nothing will reveal a psychopath more quickly than reacting inappropriately to emotional trauma in others. So they try very hard to make sure that doesn't happen.

It is, of course, much easier for the psychopath when there is an immediate reward associated with accurately imitating empathy. Trump has never had difficulty appearing to empathise with a crowd of adoring fans at one of his stadium rallies and telling them exactly what he senses they want to hear. He just struggles to manage it when there is no payoff for him. There was no immediate advantage to him in understanding the trauma of 9/11 victims, hurricane survivors or victims of school shootings, so he didn't. As Howard Glick, the Pick's disease documentary maker said, he knew he *should* care about others, he just didn't. This lack of concern for the suffering of others can be even more destructive when the psychopath's day job is one that requires empathy. If your nurse ignores your suffering, or a teacher ignores victimisation and bullying because there's nothing in it for them, then caring professions suddenly become uncaring professions.

Psychopaths can pay attention to what we feel, and act appropriately, if there is immediate reward for doing so. When the reward is non-existent, or not obvious, they need to be reminded what the appropriate actions are. But no amount of practice can make them truly feel emotional empathy. They simply do not have the necessary hardware.

Are there any effective pharmaceutical treatments for psychopathy? Oxytocin and vasopressin can affect trust levels and emotional empathy in non-psychopaths, but so far trials in psychopaths have been a bust. This is because those hormones interact with the von Economo neurons which are, of course, missing in psychopaths.

7

In 1906, physiologist and Nobel Laureate Sir Henry Dale discovered that extracts from the pituitary gland could make a pregnant cat's uterus contract. He isolated the hormone responsible and named it oxytocin, Greek for 'sudden childbirth'. But oxytocin does an awful lot more than cause the uterus to contract. It is also a powerful driver of empathy.

Oxytocin is a hormone produced in our hypothalamus, the part of the brain responsible for keeping our body in a stable state by regulating things like our body temperature and heart rate. It is transmitted into our bloodstream via the pituitary gland, and into our brain by specialist neurons. Vasopressin, a very similar hormone, is produced and released using the same pathways. The two hormones act together to affect childbirth, breastmilk production, blood pressure, urine production and water intake. Oxytocin is released in particularly large amounts during and after childbirth. It is now widely used to induce or assist with labour, and to reduce bleeding after delivery. It is also used to assist in breastfeeding, as it has been shown to stimulate breastmilk production.

Oxytocin became interesting to mental health researchers in the early 1990s, when they were able to prove that breastfeeding mothers were less anxious than bottle-feeding mothers. This inspired further research in animals, which showed that the increased oxytocin levels during pregnancy and in the first month after birth led to mothers and infants forming closer bonds. Sheep could be induced to ignore their offspring by suppressing oxytocin, and virgin sheep would show maternal behaviours towards unrelated lambs after being injected with oxytocin.

Oxytocin clearly affected parental bonding, so researchers were interested to see if its effects extended to bonding before babies were involved. Was it involved in love or, as the scientists prefer to call it, pair-bonding? The answer is yes, but only in the very small subset of animal species that have von Economo neurons.

Ninety-seven per cent of mammal species do not form monogamous relationships. One of the 3 per cent who do are a type of vole called a prairie vole. Voles are rat-like mammals found in the wild in Europe and Asia. Unlike most other species of vole and all rodents usually studied in labs, prairie voles pair for life. They have lengthy mating sessions lasting up to 24 hours, then eat, nest and raise their offspring together afterwards. They also aggressively defend their partner, and avoid incest or interaction with other potential mates for the remainder of their lives. Other vole species, like most mammals, prefer one-night or, more realistically, one-minute stands with any partner capable of reproduction.

Their human-like pair-bonding makes prairie voles an interesting species for research exploring the role of oxytocin and vasopressin in social bonding. Just like humans, when prairie voles have sex, large amounts of oxytocin and vasopressin are released in the brain. When researchers have blocked that release, prairie voles behave like most other mammals. Sex is brief, and there is no sign of pair bonding. That release of oxytocin and vasopressin is clearly necessary to forming the partner bond.

And it turns out that sex is not necessary. If prairie voles are injected with oxytocin and vasopressin they will partner for life even if they don't have sex. But the same injection doesn't work for the species of vole who prefer one-minute stands. They continue being root-rats. The difference between the prairie voles and the other vole species is that, like humans, prairie voles have von Economo neurons. Injecting oxytocin and vasopressin only works to increase pair-bonding if the animal has those neurons.

Oxytocin and vasopressin clearly play a role in social bonding, but only in species that are capable of becoming partnered for life. Since humans also form partner bonds or, as we prefer to call it, fall in love, the vole studies inspired researchers to explore whether oxytocin and vasopressin had a role in human moods, bonding, trust and empathy.

Detailed studies in humans have shown that these two hormones do indeed affect human bonding. When nasal sprays containing oxytocin and vasopressin were administered, they also cause increased social awareness, empathy and trust. When researchers have administered these hormones to people playing the prisoner's dilemma game, they have observed significant changes in behaviour. Oxytocin and vasopressin supercharged cooperation, but also made us more likely to retaliate if the other person cheated. Both hormones made the subjects twice as likely to pursue a Tit for Tat strategy, our primary evolved solution to the tragedy of the commons.

These hormones sensitise us to other people's behaviour. They make us more socially aware – we care more about what other people think of us. Their presence stimulates dopamine release in our reward pathways, makes us less anxious in the short term and motivates us to do more of the thing that stimulated the oxytocin and vasopressin release.

There is now a fast-expanding field of research focused on developing drugs based on oxytocin and vasopressin for use in treating depression, anxiety, schizophrenia and even autism. Although the outcomes of that research have, so far, not been consistent, there have been some encouraging results. It was therefore logical to think that oxytocin and vasopressin administration might also have a positive effect on psychopaths, the people lacking empathy. Unfortunately, so far, the research on this has been far from conclusive. Sometimes oxytocin and vasopressin seem to make psychopaths more empathic, but sometimes they don't. And sometimes they even seem to make them worse at interpreting emotions – a particularly dangerous outcome in a population prone to solving misunderstandings with violence.

For a hormone to change an animal's behaviour, the relevant neurons need to express molecules on their surface which can receive those hormones. Von Economo neurons express receptors for vasopressin and oxytocin. Like humans, prairie voles have von Economo neuron connections in the parts of the brain involved in emotional processing. Imaging studies on prairie voles show that, unlike other species of vole, they have strong concentrations of the receptors for oxytocin and vasopressin in the parts of the brain where von Economo neurons are at their most concentrated. This is likely how these hormones influence empathy, bonding and trust. They appear to magnify our sensitivity to the emotions of others. They make us hyper-empathic and hyper-sensitive to the way others feel. Because they also do that to the other person, they increase the likelihood of high levels of trust between strangers, and make the road to love somewhat less rocky.

Injecting oxytocin and vasopressin didn't make promiscuous voles into prairie voles. Likewise, there is no convincing evidence that oxytocin or vasopressin based drugs have any positive effect on psychopathy. That is because psychopathy is a hardware failure. Or, more precisely, psychopaths, just like promiscuous vole species, lack von Economo neurons, the circuitry for empathy. In people who have that circuitry, oxytocin and vasopressin may enhance their capacity for empathy. In people without that circuitry, these hormones have no effect at all. You might fall in love with a psychopath, but they can't fall in love with you, no matter how much oxytocin you make them sniff.

Are there any other drugs that affect empathy? The answer is yes, but not in a good way. Oxytocin and vasopressin injection may have no effect on empathy in psychopaths, but there is another very common drug, paracetamol, that has a significant effect on emotional empathy. The bad news is, that effect is to make non-psychopaths less empathic and less trusting. The good news is that it can't make a psychopath more psychopathic.

8

Acetaminophen is known as Tylenol in the United States and paracetamol or Panadol in the rest of the world. It occupies an unusual and unique position among pharmaceuticals: it is the only over-the-counter drug, with billions of doses sold annually, that is also a powerful toxin. It is also the only empathy-suppressing drug taken regularly by a significant percentage of the world's population.

Its mild pain and fever relieving properties were first recognised in 1889, but it wasn't marketed due to misplaced concerns that it caused methemoglobinemia, a condition that impairs oxygen transport in the bloodstream. It was rediscovered in 1949 and released as a painkiller in Britain under the brand name Panadol in 1956. In the US it was sold as Children's Tylenol in 1955, and in Australia it appeared as paracetamol a year later. In all three countries you needed a prescription to buy it until 1960, when it became an over-the-counter medication. It instantly became popular in the UK and Australia, not least because it was perceived to be a safer alternative to aspirin, particularly for children and people with ulcers. It took longer to catch on in the US, but in the early 1980s an association between aspirin consumption and Reye's syndrome, a brain-swelling condition in children, was reported and the paracetamol market exploded. Paracetamol became the main pain and fever medication for children. Reye's syndrome only affected children, but the suggestion of harm drove massive growth in the paracetamol market for adults as well.

Obviously, as it says on the box, paracetamol suppresses physical pain. But a 2010 study showed it worked well on emotional pain, too. A team working across six US universities set up an experiment to determine if paracetamol affected how we perceived the pain of social rejection. In the trial, undergraduate students were randomly assigned to a group taking daily paracetamol or a placebo for three weeks. Each day they were all asked to complete a scientific questionnaire designed to measure whether they had experienced social exclusion that day. They were asked to rate their degree of hurt from one to five in answer to statements like 'Today, being teased hurt my feelings.' They were also asked to rate the degree of positive emotion they felt that day. The results could not have been more clear. Nothing changed for the placebo group. And nothing changed on the positive emotion scale for either group. But there was a significant reduction in hurt feelings in the group taking paracetamol. The paracetamol reduced emotional pain as well as physical pain.

In a follow-up experiment, the researchers used functional MRI scans to observe the brains of people taking either paracetamol or a placebo as they played a game in which they were excluded by people tossing a ball to each other, a standard test of social exclusion. The scans showed that, as expected, the people taking paracetamol had much less activity in the part of the frontal cortex associated with processing social rejection. In other words, when we take this drug, we care less about what others think of us. Paracetamol is not just a physical painkiller, it's an emotional painkiller too. As paracetamol doses increase, our care factor for others drops.

But here's the thing. Paracetamol not only relieves your own pain, it also stops you feeling the pain of others. The parts of the brain affected by paracetamol were the same as those coming up in Kent Kiehl's work imaging the brains of imprisoned psychopaths. It was therefore not a big leap to consider the possibility that paracetamol affected more than just hurt feelings.

In 2016, Dominik Mischkowski, a pain researcher from Ohio University, wondered whether the drug might also reduce positive empathy. Positive empathy is the feeling we get when something good happens to another person. It is the bread and butter of movies like *Sleepless in Seattle* and *Notting Hill* and just about every other boy-meets-girl-overcomes-obstacles-and-lives-happily-ever-after movie. Mischkowski's study produced almost identical results to the earlier studies on social exclusion: paracetamol also made us less able to experience positive empathy. The moral of the story is if you want to enjoy the emotional seesaw of *Sleepless in Seattle*, don't take paracetamol beforehand.

These studies used normal doses of paracetamol, usually two 500 mg tablets in the morning after waking. The research showed that the drug is a powerful suppressor of oxytocin and vaso-pressin, and results in a dose-dependent reduction in both negative and positive empathy. When the dose was doubled to include two tablets at night, the effect also doubled. Just as had been proven in relation to feeling the pain of rejection, the more paracetamol the subjects had, the less they cared about good things happening to other people. Paracetamol suppressed their empathy circuitry in the same way the researchers had done when they made bonded for life prairie voles act like their root-rat brethren.

Paracetamol is now the most heavily consumed over-the-counter medication in the world. In Australia, more than 60 per cent of people aged over fourteen purchase it at least once a month. In the US, about a quarter of all adults use a medication containing paracetamol at least once a week. The average US adult consumes around 300 doses of paracetamol a year.

The effects of all that empathy suppression are starting to become visible in large-scale studies. Since the late 1970s, many psychology researchers have been using a standard questionnaire to measure empathy in study populations. The Interpersonal Reactivity Index (IRI) asks the subject to answer 28 statements on a five-point scale ranging from 'Does not describe me well' to 'Describes me very well'. Examples of the statements include '4. Sometimes I don't feel very sorry for other people when they are having problems,' and '13. When I see someone get hurt, I tend to remain calm.' The IRI, with the same set of 28 statements, has been used in thousands of studies in the last four decades, and because the subjects of those studies are often US college students, it is possible to compare results from people who were the same age at the time they did the IRI but are from different birth cohorts.

In 2010, Sara Konrath from the University of Michigan decided to look at whether empathy, as measured by the IRI, had changed at all since the IRI began being used in 1979. She analysed the IRI results for 72 separate studies of American college students who had completed the test between 1979 and 2009. The analysis revealed that over four decades, average US college student empathy levels had dropped by an incredible 40 per cent, with the decline accelerating since 2000. Notably, students in 2009 were significantly less likely to agree with statements that showed a level of empathetic concern for their fellow man.

Konrath blamed the rise of social media for this drop in empathy, but her study was published six years before Mischkowski's work proved that paracetamol actively suppresses human empathy. During the 40-year period covered by Konrath's study, para-cetamol had gone from a poor second choice to aspirin to being the mainstay over-the-counter pain relief. By 2008, American consumers were purchasing over 25 billion doses without pre-scription, with the market growing by 4–5 per cent per annum. It is little wonder that Konrath was seeing plummeting empathy scores in the IRI studies.

Psychopaths are not affected by increasing the levels of oxytocin and vasopressin because they don't have the von Economo neurons necessary to receive their signals. Similarly, using paracetamol to decrease oxytocin and vasopressin will have no effect in psycho-paths. But for the rest of us, the biochemistry is very clear.

Paracetamol makes us care less about our fellow humans. It makes us less empathic. It makes us more like psychopaths.

9

Imagine for a minute that you are Karen, a programmer working on a project that is critical to your company's future. Steven, another member of the team, is struggling to get a complex algorithm to function properly. You offer to help him out and he gladly accepts. You have a reputation as a brilliant programmer, and the deadline for the project is fast approaching. You introduce flawed code that seems to work based on preliminary testing but which you know will cause the software to fail in the hands of your biggest customer. Unsuspecting, Steven happily integrates the flawed code into his work. When the project is delivered and the inevitable customer emergency occurs, you step in and fix Steven's broken code using a solution you have been holding back. The CEO is grateful to you for saving the day and publicly praises you for your problem-solving skills. Meanwhile, Steven is blamed for almost destroying one of the company's most valuable customer relationships.

To a psychopath, the world appears as a dangerous and malign place. But it also a place full of trusting fools that you can exploit if you are clever. It is a world of kill or be killed. Other people are either threats, loyal supporters or irrelevant. No-one can be trusted, and your survival depends entirely on your ability to take what others have. A world without trust is a dark place, but you have complete confidence in your ability to dominate it.

4

The key features of psychopathy

BEING AN INTRASPECIES PREDATOR

In the movie *The Invention of Lying*, Ricky Gervais plays a chubby, snub-nosed everyman, Mark Bellison. Mark lives in a world where everybody always tells the truth. A TV ad for Coke encourages the viewer to buy the obesity inducing 'brown sugar-water' because it's 'very famous'. A bus ad reminds people to ask for Pepsi 'when they don't have Coke'. A retirement home describes itself as 'A Sad Place for Hopeless Old People'.

At the start of the film, Mark is on a blind date with Jennifer, who takes a call from her mother at the table. She provides her mother with a frank assessment of how the date is going: 'Hello? Yes, I'm with him right now. No, not very attractive. No, doesn't make much money. He's all right though. Seems nice. Kind of funny. A bit fat. Funny little snub nose. No, I won't be sleeping with him tonight. Nope, probably not even a kiss. Okay, you too. Bye.'

This doesn't offend Mark. He lives in a world where people have been almost pathologically honest with him every day of his life. The date ends with Mark getting the expected peck on the cheek, but there is a glimmer of hope when Jennifer promises to assess his chances of a second date when she is sober.

Mark is a writer for a movie production company that makes unbelievably turgid films accurately recounting famous historical events using armchair narration. Fiction is impossible in a world without lying and so, of course, is acting, because that would involve pretending to be someone you aren't. Unfortunately, Mark has been unable to turn stories from the fourteenth century, his assigned genre, into box-office hits. His scripts about the Black Death have been particularly depressing and unsuccessful, so he is fired without ceremony. As he leaves the office, he checks his email and finds a message from Jennifer letting him know that she has considered his looks, financial situation and his position in life and decided she is too far out of his league, and so has no interest in him romantically. The day gets worse when Mark is evicted from his apartment. The rent is $800, but he truthfully tells the landlord he has only $300 in his account. The landlord helps him move his stuff into the corridor and suggests he use the $300 to hire a truck to remove it from the building.

Mark heads to the bank to withdraw his $300, but all the stress makes something in his brain snap, causing him to 'say something that wasn't'. In a world without lies, there isn't a word for lying. He asks the teller for $800, even though the computer says he only has $300. The teller believes Mark, because people never lie. She gives him the money and warns her co-workers that the computer is a 'bit buggy' today. Mark quickly discovers he can say anything he likes and he will be believed. Later, in the bar, he demonstrates his newfound talent to his friends by telling them lies. He says he is black. They respond that he's very light-skinned but they can see it. He tells them he's an Eskimo and they say they've never seen a black Eskimo. He tells them he's a one-armed Jewish space explorer and they ask about his launch date and how he lost his arm.

Mark's world is obviously an exaggeration, but it does contain a grain of truth. Humans default to trust. Our default position is to be honest until the other person isn't, and then retaliate in kind until they are honest again. We can't tell bank tellers we have $800 in the bank when we only have $300 and expect the teller to believe us, but most people will take us at face value until we give them a reason not to trust us. And if someone betrays our trust, we will bounce back to being nice if we believe they have too. When Mark discovers lying, it must be similar to how a psychopath feels when they first learn that most of us trust others by default.

Mark discovers that the rest of the world is at a distinct disadvantage because they always tell the truth. He, on the other hand, is unshackled. He can say whatever he likes and be believed. This is how the real world looks to a psychopath. To them, it is populated by disabled fools – us – who trust at first sight. In the real world, the psychopath must be a little more cautious, because we are not playing 'trust everybody all the time', we are playing Tit for Tat. If we spot deception, we will probably retaliate. But for as long as a psychopath does nothing to alarm us, he can say whatever he likes and we will still believe him. The opportunities are endless.

One of the most common places psychopaths lie is on their resumes. They will happily fabricate credentials and work history, using carefully disguised lies. They will thoroughly research the companies, clients and projects they falsely claim to have been involved with to ensure their lies are consistent with real-world information. By carefully crafting their lies to include elements of truth or to ensure they are difficult to verify, they will make it challenging for anyone to disprove their claims. For example, they may claim to have worked with a high-profile client who values their privacy, making it less likely for others to question the details of their collaboration. Psychopaths are skilled at thinking on their feet and adapting their lies to fit changing circumstances. If confronted with new information or inconsistencies in their story, they can quickly come up with plausible explanations to maintain the facade. Because we default to trust, when doubt arises we will usually be inclined to believe what the psychopath is telling us.

Mark decides to see what his superpower can do for him. Walking down the street, he sees a gorgeous blonde who tells him to stop staring at her because she doesn't find him attractive. He races after her and tells her that if she doesn't have sex with him the world will end. The blonde is traumatised by the prospect of the world ending and, after establishing that they have time to get inside rather than doing it in the street, accompanies Mark to a motel. As she tries to remove her clothes while bawling her eyes out, Mark is overcome with remorse. He takes a fake call from

NASA, who apparently advise him that the world is no longer in danger and she is free to go.

This is a key departure from a real-world psychopath. If Mark were truly a psychopath, he would have had sex with the blonde. He would use her default state of trust to benefit himself. Psychopaths are not concerned about what other people feel. They cannot feel other people's emotions, so those emotions are not a consideration. A psychopath would not worry that the lie he had told caused the girl emotional distress. The point is that he got to have sex with her. Most of us have a similar attitude to plant life. Perhaps the grass in my lawn has feelings about me running a mower over it, and perhaps it doesn't. My von Economo neurons are not picking up any emotions from the lawn, and so I don't factor them into my decision-making. I am happy to assume that cutting the grass doesn't affect it. The more the life form we are interacting with behaves like a human, the more inclined we are to take its feelings into account. Most of us don't worry too much about the feelings of ants and spiders, but we care quite a bit about dogs. Some people even care about cats.

A psychopath can feel regret if their actions result in them suffering harm themselves, but cannot feel remorse for the effect their actions have on other people, any more than you would feel remorse for mowing the lawn. They simply do not have the wiring to care what you feel. If a psychopath had had sex with the blonde, but contracted herpes, he would regret it. But the girl's feelings do not factor into that equation. If I am injured while mowing the lawn, I'll regret it, but I still won't feel any remorse for what the grass might feel about being cut.

In a psychopath's world, the only emotions that matter are their own. This is fundamental to the character of a psychopath, and the key to understanding everything they do. They know you experience emotions, but they cannot feel them, and so they do not automatically take them into account. Other people's emotions are something they have to *choose* to notice and then, if necessary, adjust for. Emotional blindness is something they see as a super-power, while we see it as a mental illness.

There is, however, a downside to this 'superpower'. Unlike Mark, a real-world psychopath cannot be sure that everyone else is always telling the truth. Yes, we default to being nice, but not always, and not in all circumstances. We are nowhere near as reliable as the man selling brown sugar-water in the TV adver-tisement. The reason we evolved empathy was to assist in deciding whether we could trust other people. It is a sixth sense that is part lie detector and part behaviour moderator. It helps us detect and incorporate, as if they were our own, the other person's emotions into our decision-making. It stops us lying in most situations because we assume the other person also has functional empathy. If they do, we are safe to assume they will not harm us.

A psychopath is not 'impaired' by empathetic emotional feedback. This means a psychopath cannot trust anybody. They do not have the wiring for trust, so while they can be pretty sure we will be honest most of the time, they cannot know that for sure.

How do psychopaths make us trust them? Charm. While we may sense their lack of empathy, they charm us into ignoring the alarm bells.

Hervey Cleckley identified superficial charm as a primary characteristic of psychopathy, and it is included in all modern diagnostic checklists. Psychopaths can be extraordinarily charming. They use that charm to allay any doubts we may intuitively have about their motives. To a psychopath, charm is a smokescreen that allows them to get on with cheating while delaying or defusing our reaction to that cheating.

Arnold Toynbee, one of Britain's best-known historians and an expert on international affairs, met with Adolf Hitler in 1936 and came away with an immensely positive impression. He reported in a confidential memorandum to the Prime Minister that he was 'convinced of [his] sincerity in desiring peace in Europe and close friendship with England'. In the same year, former British Prime Minister Lloyd George spent hours in a private meeting with Hitler. Afterwards, he was gushing in his praise, saying, 'Hitler is one of the greatest men . . . He is a born leader of men. A magnetic and dynamic personality with a single-minded purpose, a resolute will and a dauntless heart.' Similarly, then British Prime Minister Neville Chamberlain, just months before the outbreak of the Second World War, left a private one-on-one meeting with Hitler saying he was 'a man who could be relied on when he had given his word'. Hitler had promised Chamberlain that Britain and Germany would never go to war again. He had even signed a piece of paper with words to that effect. On his return to Britain, Chamberlain refused to put industry on a war footing for fear of suggesting to Hitler that he would abandon their agreement. Five months later, Hitler invaded Czechoslovakia.

Donald Trump's niece Mary is a clinical psychologist and the author of *Too Much and Never Enough: How My Family Created the World's Most Dangerous Man*, released in 2020. Mary is not a fan of her famous uncle. In the book she shares a brief anecdote which gives an insight into one of the most powerful tools in a psychopath's armoury: charm.

It was 2017 and Mary had been invited to a family get-together at the White House. The freshly inaugurated President stood in the doorway personally greeting each guest as they arrived. Mary writes, '[W]hen he saw me, he pointed at me with a surprised look on his face, then said, "I specifically asked for you to be here."' He then opened his arms and hugged her for the first time in her life. 'That was the kind of thing he often said to charm people,' Mary wrote, 'and he had a knack for tailoring his comment to the occasion, which was all the more impressive because I know it wasn't true.'

Others who have met Trump in person have had similar experiences. When the heads of the world's largest pharmaceutical companies were invited to the White House in early 2017, they were not expecting an enjoyable experience. Trump had spent weeks attacking them on social media, accusing them of 'getting away with murder' by overcharging for life-saving medicines. Their stock prices had been slammed as a result, costing shareholders billions. To their surprise, they found Trump to be a genial host who gave them personal guided tours of the White House and the Oval Office and didn't once suggest they were at fault for the cost of drugs. Instead, he talked about outdated regulations driving up their costs and his plans to help them by streamlining the law. Trump listened rather than lectured, and they came away feeling he had heard their concerns and was there to help them.

This was not a unique experience. During 2017, Reuters News Agency interviewed nearly a dozen executives and lobbyists who had taken part in similar meetings. When Trump hosted a meeting of US car manufacturers, he playfully tapped General Motors CEO Mary Barra on the shoulder and gently asked her to add more local jobs. Later, according to the video transcript, he pulled out her chair for her as the meeting started. At the same meeting, he greeted Ford CEO Mark Fields with 'Happy Birthday. It's his birthday ladies and gentlemen.' He also said it was a 'great honor' to see Fiat Chrysler CEO Sergio Marchionne. Mary Barra was so impressed that she mentioned the meeting in a speech she gave a month later, saying Trump 'really listened' to the car makers' concerns. Despite his Twitter commentary costing the companies a fortune in lost share market capital, most supported Trump after private meetings with him. In person, Donald Trump was charming and cajoling. He was not the vicious public persona that slammed the same companies on Twitter.

Trump knows something that every clothing store assistant knows, and that psychologists have repeatedly proven: flattery will get you everywhere. We are more likely to trust someone who flatters us. One of the seminal works in the area is a 1978 study by a team from the University of North Carolina. The subjects spoke to a person, the evaluator, who needed a favour for someone else. The evaluator would insert positive, negative or mixed comments about the subject in the conversation. When they received positive comments, the subjects were much more likely to trust the evaluator and help them. This remained true even when the subjects were made aware that the flatterers would personally profit from the favour. The accuracy of the flattery didn't matter either. Even when the flatterer said something that the subject knew to be an exaggeration or just plain false, they still liked the flatterer more, and were more likely to cooperate.

To a psychopath, the world is full of people you can never trust. You need to count your change at the supermarket. You need to check that the mechanic did what he said he would do. Because you assume everybody thinks the same way you do, you are extremely paranoid. You cannot understand how anyone else could trust you, so you assume they will betray you given half a chance. But you also know that if you turn on the charm, you have a better chance of them trusting you. This is why victims of psychopaths often report being charmed by the psychopath when they first met. If a psychopath compliments you, they want you to trust them. Psychopaths are good listeners. They listen to what you say is important to you and they reflect that back to you. Chamberlain wanted Hitler to tell him there would be no war, so that's what Hitler told him. Then to ice the cake, they throw in a little flattery. For many people this is enough to make them trust the psychopath, no matter how they have previously behaved.

How can a psychopath have any kind of relationship if they don't trust the other person? Well, they can, it's just not a relationship you'd want to be in. Because a psychopath cannot trust you, they need to control you. That means for as long as they need a relationship with you, they will try to force your loyalty with rewards and punishment.

2

In his 1999 biography, John A Byrne described Albert 'Chainsaw Al' Dunlap, the notorious former CEO of Sunbeam, as a person who 'sucked the very life and soul out of companies and people. He stole dignity, purpose, and sense out of organizations and replaced those ideals with fear and intimidation.' Dunlap was known for his aggressive cost-cutting measures, including significant layoffs and plant closures. His methods were destructive and damaging to companies' long-term prospects. In Byrne's view, Dunlap focused solely on immediate financial gains at the expense of employees, company culture, and sustainable growth. By the time Byrne's book was published, its subject was under investigation for fraud and infamous for his corporate tactics, which usually involved a lot of people losing their jobs.

Dunlap seemed to enjoy firing people so much that in 2005, *Fast Company* magazine had included him in its list of potentially psychopathic CEOs. Almost a decade later, author Jon Ronson interviewed Al. Ronson had convinced Dunlap to take Robert Hare's psychopathy test as part of the research for his book, *The Psychopath Test*. Chainsaw Al readily admitted to most of the criteria for psychopathy, but to his mind, these characteristics were signs of a good leader. Being impulsive meant he was a quick decision-maker. A lack of empathy meant he was not affected by 'nonsense emotions'. And he saw his lack of remorse as allowing him to move forward to do more great things. To Dunlap, being manipulative was being inspirational. He couldn't understand how a grandiose sense of self-worth and superficial charm could be bad things. And other people's suffering piqued his curiosity, rather than causing him to feel shock or inspiring a desire to help.

Dunlap believed he lived in a kill or be killed world. In his autobiography, *Mean Business*, he explained, 'The predators are out there, circling, trying to stare you down, waiting for any sign of weakness, ready to pounce and make you their next meal.' Al's paranoia is a common trait in those congenitally unable to trust others. Donald Trump operated on a similar philosophy. In 1981, he told *People* magazine, 'Man is the most vicious of all animals, and life is a series of battles ending in victory or defeat.' And both men could have been, but probably weren't, quoting Niccolo Machiavelli, the sixteenth-century Italian statesman, who said, 'It is that men feed upon each other, and those who cannot defend themselves must be worried.' Machiavelli literally wrote the book on how to be a psychopath. *The Prince* is a manual for aspiring government officials, and probably the most famous book on political philosophy ever written. In it, Machiavelli says the only way to get ahead in life is to use force or fraud and then pretend you didn't. The word 'Machiavellian', meaning to be cunning, duplicitous or unscrupulous, is often used as a synonym for psychopathy.

Albert John Dunlap graduated from West Point in 1960, 537th in a class of 550. He served as a paratrooper at a nuclear missile site before signing on as a management trainee at a Kimberly-Clark paper mill in 1963. He held a variety of executive jobs in the paper industry over the following decade, eventually landing a job as Chief Operating Officer of Nitec, a Niagara Falls paper mill employing 700 people. It was quite a coup, given he'd been fired by his previous employer, Max Phillips & Son, a small paper plant, for neglecting his duties and speaking so badly about his boss that he had hurt the company's business. He'd lasted just two months into a three-year contract, with constant complaints from staff about his 'snarling temper'.

It took Dunlap six months to find the job at Nitec. But the company's chair, George S Petty, was charmed by him and supported his approach to business. Dunlap's task was to reverse the fortunes of the struggling company. To achieve this, he immediately started firing people. As a result of Dunlap's cost-cutting efforts, the firm managed to report small profits in 1975 and 1976.

Regarding himself a successful pillar of the business community, Dunlap joined the local country club and began challenging members to tennis matches. He quickly ran out of opposition because he was a spectacular cheat who would fly into a rage if the opponent challenged him. Cheating is something psychopaths do as a matter of course. Donald Trump, for example, persistently cheats at golf by improving the lie of his ball. He is reputed to kick the ball so often the caddies nicknamed him 'Pele', after one of the greatest soccer players of all time. Bryan Marsal, chair of the 2020 Men's US Open Golf tournament and Trump's frequent playing companion, explained to *Golf* magazine that Trump believes 'you're gonna cheat him' so is unapologetic about doing so.

When psychopaths play the prisoner's dilemma, they tend to rat out their co-conspirator. A person without von Economo neurons cannot trust the other not to cheat. They assume that person thinks the same way they do, and will rat them out. And if the other person doesn't cheat, they will get an advantage – giving them even more reason to cheat. Cheating is obvious in tests like the prisoner's dilemma and social sports that rely on the honesty of the players, but that doesn't bother psychopaths, because they assume everyone is taking the same approach. To a psychopath's mind, if everybody's cheating, it's not really cheating. Someone who compulsively and regularly cheats at games is likely to also be cheating in more complex situations. A tendency to cheat is hard-wired into the brain of a psychopath. They simply cannot understand why someone wouldn't do so, and consider people who don't cheat to be fools.

In August 1976, Petty abruptly fired Dunlap because, it was later revealed in court filings, virtually all the senior managers below Dunlap had threatened to resign, *en masse*, if he remained. Nonetheless, given the company was about to report a $5 million annual profit, Petty arranged a substantial bonus payment to Dunlap on his departure. Shortly after Dunlap left, external auditors discovered the expected profit would in fact be a $5.5 million loss. The auditors found expenses that had not been included in the accounts, overstated inventory and made-up sales. Petty immediately cancelled the bonus arrangement, sparking years of litigation with Dunlap which ultimately bankrupted Nitec.

After Nitec, Dunlap got a job in strategic planning at American Can, a fading tin-can manufacturer, then the Manville Corporation, an asbestos miner and timber miller. Dunlap was fired within the year, but was then recruited to save Lily-Tulip, a large paper cup manufacturer struggling to survive after a leveraged buyout. He 'saved' it by firing almost all the senior managers on his first day at work, halving head office staff and firing a fifth of the rest. He offloaded what remained in 1986, netting himself a $6 million windfall in the process. During his time at Lily-Tulip, Dunlap had a small bronze sculpture of four sharks in a feeding frenzy on his desk. He said it was to remind him that the world is full of sharks.

Dunlap's caustic but successful style attracted the attention of corporate raider Sir James Goldsmith, who recruited him to assist in a failed attempt to take over British American Tobacco, and then in the successful acquisition of Crown Zellerbach, a pulp and paper company Goldsmith had purchased as a hostile takeover in 1985. Dunlap implemented his usual plan to cut costs. He fired a fifth of the staff and renegotiated the employment contracts of the remainder.

On Goldsmith's recommendation, Kerry Packer hired Dunlap to sort out Consolidated Press Holdings in 1991. Packer wanted some liquidity after suffering a massive heart attack the previous year. Dunlap set to work cutting staff and operations. He told the Packers to stay out of his way, and they did. One of his first tasks was to get Packer's giant US subsidiary, Valassis, which printed savings coupons inserted into papers, ready for sale. David Brandon, the president of Valassis at the time, said working for Dunlap was a 'living hell'. According to Brandon, Dunlap was a power monger and a control freak who enjoyed sacking people. Dunlap's strategy was designed to get his way. He would isolate people, then eviscerate them in meetings. Two years into the job and three years before his contract was up, Dunlap was summarily fired by Packer. No reason was ever given. After Chainsaw Al left, it took Packer four years to stabilise Valassis to the point where it could be sold.

Dunlap's control strategies are common to almost all detailed reports of psychopathic behaviour in workplaces. In June 2013, Associate Professor Clive Boddy from Anglia Ruskin University encountered an executive of a large UK charity who was convinced his new CEO was a psychopath. Boddy, a leading expert in corporate psychopathy, convinced the executive to participate in a case study of his CEO, giving a series of detailed interviews. The case study provides detailed insight into the strategies the psychopath used to control the charity.

Boddy reports on the psychopath's strategy of isolation and punishment, citing the example of a female senior manager who the psychopathic CEO decided to target. The respondent reported, 'He walked (all) over her in meetings, wouldn't allow her to speak to other managers when they had board meetings and so on and talked over her and made her life a living hell until, bless her, she decided the best thing for her to do was to sign a compromise agreement and leave.' Ultimately, the CEO's strategy resulted in most of the managers resigning over a three-year period. Their replacements were, of course, hired by the psychopath, and were invariably people who understood he prized loyalty above competence. Of the four remaining senior managers, the respondent said one was settling into retirement and uninterested in anything challenging and two of the others were 'completely useless'.

Psychopaths can't trust others to work with them to achieve the psychopath's goals. But they know that most of us are motivated by the anticipation of punishment. Psychopaths have spent a lifetime learning what psychologists proved with their fearlessness tests: when non-psychopaths know a punishment is coming, they become anxious and change their behaviour. Psychopaths know they don't need to punish all of us. It is enough to choose a victim, like the female manager in the UK charity, and publicly execute them, figuratively speaking, to keep the rest of us in line. They know the fear of the same thing happening to us will bend us to their will. Then they don't need to trust us – they know we will comply out of fear. Of course, this doesn't work on other psychopaths, but there are trust-free solutions for handling them too.

After being dismissed by Packer, Dunlap landed the CEO role at Scott Paper, the oldest and largest US manufacturer of toilet paper. The company was heavily in debt and had depressed earnings. Dunlap was brought in to turn it around. He immediately sacked eight of the eleven senior executives and replaced them with people he had previously worked with, who he knew would do as he said. He then ditched three-quarters of the headquarters staff and fired 11,000 workers, about a third of the company's staff. Most of the people fired were gone within a week. Dunlap then arranged huge stock option distributions to all the middle and upper managers who remained. Those options were worth much more if the company was sold quickly, so they effectively became golden chains holding the executives in their jobs and ensuring none would challenge Dunlap's authority. Getting fired didn't just mean losing your job, it meant losing millions in options as well.

If Al told you to jump, you asked 'how high?' Chainsaw Al still didn't trust anyone, but had now added potential reward as a means of keeping people in line. Psychopaths are less receptive to punishment, so if there were any other psychopaths in the senior management ranks, the golden chains would be more effective at motivating them.

A year later Dunlap sold off the remains of Scott Paper for $9.4 billion, pocketing a $100 million payout for his trouble. After the purchase, the buyer, Kimberly-Clark, found that the costs had been cut so deeply that the equipment had fallen into disrepair and the inventory channels were full of goods sold off on the cheap. It took three years to undo the damage. Of course, that wasn't Dunlap's problem. By then, he'd moved on to become the CEO of Sunbeam appliances.

When Dunlap arrived at Sunbeam in 1996 he granted huge stock option entitlements to the top 300 executives, having learned the value of golden chains at Scott Paper. The grants were twice the size of the industry average, but vested over three years. The executives were now effectively automatons at his control. He didn't need to trust anyone. Dunlap treated the senior management just as badly as he did everyone else. According to Richard Boynton, president of the household products division, he was condescending, belligerent and disrespectful. But he had purchased the execs' loyalty, and they set about executing his plan to fire half the 12,000 staff and eliminate 87 per cent of the company's products.

Sunbeam managers described working for Chainsaw Al as being like trench warfare. The pressure was brutal, and the casualties were high. Dunlap set impossibly high revenue goals and then placed his direct reports under extreme pressure to meet them. They in turn pressured those who worked for them. And all down the line, people were summarily fired if they didn't produce the numbers. In a desperate attempt to keep their jobs, people started leaving suppliers unpaid, stuffing the channels with inventory, providing endless credit to retailers and employing many other dubious tactics. Although it worked initially, it wasn't long before reality caught up with Dunlap's unreasonable goals. The board fired him in June 1998 for failing to meet his earnings projections. Even so, Dunlap successfully forced them to pay out his generous severance. Shareholders sued over the dodgy earnings projections and eventually Sunbeam was forced into bankruptcy. The Securities and Exchange Commission came after Dunlap, alleging accounting fraud. The case was settled with a $500,000 fine and Dunlap's agreement to never again work as an officer or director.

For four decades, Dunlap tore a path through corporate America. In his wake he left thousands of destroyed careers and many iconic companies either bankrupted or on life-support. Why did people keep hiring him? The answer is simple: he lied and they trusted him. He scrubbed previous employers from his resume and told people what they wanted to hear about the rest. Sunbeam and Scott Paper were significant US companies, so of course, they used well-regarded executive search firms to find and recommend Dunlap. Al's time with Max Phillips, Nitec and Manville had been left out of his employment history, but the professional recruiters missed the holes. The boards they reported to wanted to see a famous cost-cutter who turned failing businesses around, and that was the story Chainsaw Al sold them. They accepted his account of his employment history, despite publicly accessible evidence that he had worked at other places.

Had the executive firms noticed this and investigated, they may not have found much to include in their reports. People like Nitec chair George Petty, who were intimately involved, were afraid to speak up for fear of being sued. Even after the spectacular failure of Sunbeam, Dunlap continued to be evasive about his past. In the 2014 edition of his autobiography, *Mean Business*, almost everything about Sunbeam had been removed.

Why do psychopaths micromanage and bully? They think they are infallible. Their brains are incapable of valuing the thoughts or feelings of others, and they are equally incapable of learning from their own failures. As a result, they truly believe they live in a world of ignorant fools and that they are only people capable of making a decision about anything. Fortunately, they have never made a bad decision.

3

According to a psychopath, the rest of us should be loyal and unquestioning sheep. The psychopath is the all-knowing shepherd, and the only one capable of making decisions. The psychopath neither needs nor seeks input from the sheep. All he requires is that the sheep do as they are told. And since sheep cannot be trusted to do that, the psychopath needs to employ punishment and reward to keep them in line. Sure, this may result in the loss of a few sheep, but such is the cost of ensuring compliance.

Boddy's UK charity psychopath CEO thought discussion was a complete waste of time. Prior to meetings he would prepare what he called 'discussion papers'. During the meeting people would be asked if they had read the paper and if they agreed with it. If a manager agreed, the meeting moved on without discussion. If the manager disagreed, they were told that was how it was going to be, and the meeting moved on without discussion.

The psychopath CEO's need for control was so great that he couldn't tolerate a manager disagreeing even if they nevertheless complied. One manager described an occasion where he told the CEO he disagreed with a proposed course of action. The CEO responded that he had made the decision to do it regardless, adding, 'You've got to agree with me because I am the boss.' The manager pointed out that while he certainly had to do what the boss said, he didn't have to agree with it. The CEO slammed his hand on the table, raised his voice in open office and said, 'You have to agree with me', then stormed off to his desk.

This desire for absolute control extended to every small decision in the office. The manager involved in the study reported that, 'The controlling is very much an everyday occurrence. Complete interference with the minutiae of detail.' If you can't trust anyone, you need to make sure they are all doing what you want them to do, exactly the way you would do it. Experts in leadership call this 'micromanagement'.

When you are the President of the world's only superpower, you can delegate every task to teams of experts in every conceivable area. This frees you up to do the strategic, big-picture thinking required of the world's most powerful leader. But one of the hallmarks of Trump's term in office was his constant need to micromanage. He worked up options for the paint colours on Air Force One. He obsessed over the design of the wall at the US–Mexico border, getting involved in materials selection, paint colour, the number and size of doors and even the width of the slats. He would wake engineers in the middle of the night to fill them in on his latest thoughts, such as his view that the wall should be intimidating but good-looking, or that the slats should be black to absorb heat, making them hotter and harder to climb.

He even famously tried to micromanage the weather. On 1 September 2019, Trump incorrectly said that Hurricane Dorian would impact Alabama. After residents reacted in alarm, the Weather Bureau issued a statement that directly contradicted Trump, assuring the people of Alabama they were not in the path of the hurricane. Trump then spent a week publicly insisting his forecast of the hurricane's path was correct. He even produced a map on which someone had extended the path with a black marker to include Alabama. Trump denied any involvement in 'Sharpiegate', but continued to refer to maps he had found from other agencies which showed Alabama would be hit. They didn't show that at all, but it didn't stop Trump obsessing over the issue until he managed to force the National Oceanic and Atmospheric Administration to publish an unsigned statement supporting Trump's claim. A later investigation found that the head of the NOAA had violated scientific integrity codes of conduct by caving in to the demand from the White House. Unable to accept he had made a mistake, the President of the United States spent a week obsessing over weather forecasts, eventually bullying an independent agency into saying he'd been right all along. By the way, Hurricane Dorian did not strike Alabama.

This was not the first time Trump had obsessed about hurricanes. During a briefing in 2017, experts had pointed out that hurricanes that eventually make landfall in the US form off the coast of Africa. Trump replied, 'I got it. I got it. Why don't we nuke them?' His thinking was that a bomb dropped in the eye when they were forming would disrupt the hurricane. The idea wasn't original – it had first been floated in the 1940s, but had been repeatedly dismissed as unlikely to work, in violation of international treaties on the use of nuclear weapons and likely to result in radiation being distributed worldwide. That did not stop Trump raising 'his idea' with weather experts on multiple occasions during his administration.

Micromanagement was not a new feature of Trump's personality. Blanche Sprague, a high-ranking executive in Trump's private construction business, told the *Guardian* about late-night calls she would receive from Trump, such as the time he rang to tell her there was an empty soda bottle on the street in front of Trump Plaza in New York. She had to make sure it was picked up immediately. Sprague said Trump involved himself in every decision about every building the firm built. No decision was too small – from curtain colours to toilet seat size, Trump made the call. Sprague saw this as a positive, but it could easily be regarded as wildly inefficient micromanagement.

Many commentators have viewed these examples and many, many more as evidence of Trump being egomaniacal, but the science suggests this isn't really the right interpretation.

Trump's obsession about Hurricane Dorian was not about proving that he was right. It was about his inability to accept that he could be wrong. He did not care what the sheep thought but, convinced he was incapable of making an incorrect decision, it was about doing other people's jobs, in this case weather forecasters', until they also made the correct decision. It is a subtle but important distinction. It is too easy to dismiss a psychopath as an egomaniacal narcissist when in fact they are trying to bend reality to match a decision they have already made.

Because psychopaths have no negative feedback loops, they can never believe their decisions are wrong. If for some reason reality proves them to be wrong, there must be something wrong with reality. This is why, in combination with their inability to trust anyone, they need to get involved in the detail of other people's jobs.

If they are so busy doing your job, how do psychopaths have the time to do what they are supposed to be doing? The answer is their real job takes very little time due to their lack of impulse control, total confidence in their infallibility and their inability to learn from mistakes. They make decisions in a heartbeat that would take a normal person weeks or even months to make.

4

Late in the evening of 6 October 2019 President Trump called Turkish President Recep Tayyip Erdoğan. The call had been arranged to smooth the Turkish President's ruffled feathers after being denied a one-on-one meeting with Trump at the September meeting of the UN General Assembly in New York. Trump had met with a dozen world leaders during the session but said he didn't have time to meet with Erdoğan. The Turkish President had made it known that he was not happy. Erdoğan wanted to discuss creating a safe zone in northern Syria. The area was then occupied by the SDP, Kurdish forces that Turkey viewed as terrorists. The SDP had fought for almost a decade, with the support of the US military, against ISIS, the terrorist organisation responsible for major atrocities worldwide. The war had cost over 11,000 Kurdish lives, but by 2019 had resulted in the defeat of ISIS forces in Syria and Iraq. There were approximately 1000 US troops stationed in the SDP-occupied border area that Erdoğan wanted to take over as a safe zone. There were no plans for the US troops to depart, and this was in the way of Erdoğan's ambitions. The US and Turkey are NATO allies, so Turkey could not be seen to attack US forces in the area.

No-one knows for sure what happened in that phone call, but by the end of it Trump, in a complete reversal of a decade of US mid-east policy, had assured Erdoğan that the US forces in Syria would leave immediately. Erdoğan took this as a green light for invasion. Within hours, US forces were instructed to withdraw without any plan to protect the retreating troops. They had to destroy their own headquarters to prevent the arms and ammunition stored there falling into the hands of the fighters backed by Turkey. The Kurdish allies were completely abandoned, the ISIS prisoners they were guarding escaped and Iran and Russia immediately moved to increase their military influence in the region.

Trump's rash decision caught the White House, the Republican Party, the US military, its foreign policy experts and European allies completely by surprise. Trump had previously floated the idea of withdrawing from Syria. In response, then Secretary of Defense, respected General Jim Mattis, had resigned in protest. Shortly afterwards, senior members of the national security team apparently managed to convince Trump to reverse the decision. But despite appearing to drop the idea, clearly he had not actually changed his mind. In one impulsive moment Trump sacrificed the lives of thousands of fighters who had carried the fight against the world's most dangerous terrorist organisation for a decade, sent a strong message to other allies that the US could not be trusted, freed thousands of ISIS terrorists and ceded the Middle East to Iranian and Russian forces, not to mention putting US lives at risk in a shambolic withdrawal.

Nobody thought it was a good idea. Democratic Senator Jack Reed, long-serving member of the Armed Services Committee, commented, 'This president keeps blindsiding our military and diplomatic leaders and partners with impulsive moves like this that benefit Russia and authoritarian regimes.' Even Republican Senator Lindsey Graham, one of Trump's strongest allies, said at the time, 'The President is not listening. This decision and line of thinking is against all sound military advice.' He went on to say that the decision would ensure that ISIS would recover, and that it was a 'stain on America's honor for abandoning the Kurds'.

Trump acknowledged he was 'an island of one' on the move, but this did not appear to concern him. He thought it was a 'strategically brilliant' decision, evidently convinced he knew more about Syria than the generals or foreign policy experts. Trump had long considered himself a foreign policy expert. After his first meeting with Russian President Vladimir Putin in 2017 he said his years in real estate had sharpened his 'gut feel' for how to deal with foreign leaders. 'Foreign policy is what I'll be remembered for,' he claimed.

In late 2018, Trump told the *Washington Post*, 'My gut tells me more sometimes than anybody else's brain can ever tell me.' That kind of certainty is common in all psychopaths. Chainsaw Al told Jon Ronson that what Ronson was calling impulsivity was just another way of saying 'quick analysis'. 'Some people spend a week weighing up the pros and cons. Me? I look at it in ten minutes. And if the pros outweigh the cons? Go!' Psychopaths lack impulse control. They also lack any sense of doubt about their decision-making. As a result, they do not fear the consequences of a wrong decision. This is, in part, because they don't believe there will be any negative consequences for them. Decision-making is easy and quick if you can always go with your first impulse and be confident that you will never be wrong.

How do psychopaths make decisions? They will always choose the option that directly benefits them. When you or I make a decision, we weigh the consequences. If it is a big decision, we might seek expert advice, perform detailed analysis and think long and hard before committing to a position. But to a psychopath, the choice is always easy, and the only question to answer is 'Which option personally benefits me more?'

Imagine you are Gary the psychopathic corporate lawyer. You have been approached by two clients, both with high-stakes cases, but you only have the time and resources to take on one. The first client is a well-connected entrepreneur, involved in a complicated intellectual property dispute. Securing a favourable outcome for this client would leave you well-positioned to establish a long-term professional relationship with the entrepreneur, potentially benefiting from their extensive network. The second prospective client is a powerful company suing a whistleblower who disclosed massive fraud in the company's environmental compliance disclosures. According to the whistleblower, the company has been poisoning the water supply with toxic heavy metals and fabricating test results to conceal this fact. Your prospective client wants to defend the case by destroying the reputation of the whistleblower. The case has attracted widespread media attention, and a victory would catapult you into the limelight, earning you fame and recognition as a top corporate lawyer.

After carefully weighing your options, you would decide to represent the company suing the whistleblower, reasoning that the immediate benefits of fame and recognition outweigh the potential risks and long-term rewards of the entrepreneur's case. Your decision would focus solely on which case would bring you the most significant personal advantage most immediately. You would not consider the ethical implications of either case, or the potential impact on the people involved. Your psychopathy allows you to make a calculated decision based entirely on self-interest, regardless of any broader consequences.

For months prior to Trump's hasty decision on Syria, the line that got the most applause at Trump campaign rallies had been 'bring them home'. That meant for Trump, a year out from the election, the decision to do so was easy: pulling the troops out would make him more popular with his supporters. The deaths of thousands of allies, the possible resurgence of ISIS and the loss of US influence in the Middle East were all irrelevant compared to the promise of him winning votes. Psychopaths are the lonely shepherd surrounded by sheep. Asking them to care about anything but themselves would strike them as ridiculous.

5

There is a runaway tram barrelling towards five people, who are unaware of its approach. You have no way of warning them, but you can control a switch that will divert the tram onto an alternate track. The problem is that on that other track there is another person who you also cannot warn. If you don't pull the switch the tram will kill five people. If you do, it will kill one person. What do you do? This is the so-called trolley problem first posed by British philosopher Philippa Foot in a paper about the ethics of abortion decisions, published in 1967. About two-thirds of us would pull the switch, reasoning it is worth sacrificing one life to save five. But what if the scenario is slightly different?

Imagine you are a doctor who needs organ transplants to save the lives of five patients. You know there is another patient in your hospital with a fracture who is a perfect match for a transplant. Other than the fracture she is perfectly healthy, and has all five of the healthy organs you need. However, if you take those donor organs she will die. Assuming you had the power to do so, would you kill her to save the lives of the other five? Researchers posing this scenario have confirmed that almost none of us would kill her to harvest her organs – which is a bit of a relief for those of us anticipating a hospital stay.

In essence, the problems are the same. Both scenarios involve sacrificing one life for five. Even if we are told the fracture patient is terminally ill and will die soon anyway, most of us still won't kill her. For some reason, two-thirds of us are happy to allow the tram to kill the chap on the tracks but will not actively kill a patient to harvest her organs. This kind of perplexing contradiction in moral reasoning has kept philosophers busy for more than half a century. They have worked up hundreds of scenarios posing similar moral dilemmas to see where and when we draw the line.

Do psychopaths answer the trolley problem differently to the rest of us? The answer is no, they generally give the same answer. They know the socially acceptable outcome is to sacrifice one for the good of many, and they don't really care anyway, since neither outcome affects them. But when researchers have tried variations of the trolley problem that involve asking empathy-deficient people to imagine a scenario where they might personally be harmed or receive a benefit, their answers diverge significantly from the rest of us.

In 2007, a team of researchers led by Michael Koenigs from the University of Iowa decided to examine the way people with damage to their prefrontal cortex, the area of the brain that is affected by psychopathy, answered a variety of moral conundrums like the trolley problem. They then compared their answers to normal control subjects. Like Pick's disease sufferers and psychopaths, the people with damage to the prefrontal cortex had diminished emotional responses, virtually no compassion, shame or guilt, and poorly regulated anger and frustration. However, they had normal levels of intelligence, memory and logical reasoning.

The researchers posed a series of moral dilemmas to the empathy-impaired and normal groups, then compared their answers. As expected, in variations of the standard trolley problem the groups did not diverge. In both groups, about two-thirds of the subjects decided kill one person to save the lives of five people. But things got interesting when the scenarios changed so the subject was able to directly benefit, or at least avoid harm.

In Scenario 17, you are told to imagine you are leading a small group of soldiers. One soldier is badly injured in a trap, which is connected to a radio that signals the enemy that it has been triggered. If you take the injured soldier with you, you and the rest of the group cannot escape. If you leave him, he will be captured and tortured, then killed. You are told you cannot take him with you, and must decide whether to shoot him dead now to prevent his capture. Just one-third of the normal controls said they would shoot him. But more than twice as many, an extraordinary 85 per cent, of the empathy-impaired group said they would pull the trigger.

In this scenario, the potential shooting victim will die anyway, but you are being asked to give him a quicker, less painful death. This is different to the fracture patient, as taking her organs offers no benefit to her. A third of us decide, given the limited choices, to let the soldier die more humanely. But the empathy-impaired people go from having no-one prepared to kill the fracture patient to 85 per cent of them being prepared to kill the injured soldier. They are more willing to conduct a mercy killing. To the empathy impaired, another person is just an object. They would logic-ally decide instant death is a preferable outcome for the injured livestock.

Scenario 19 ramps up the stakes and directly engages self-interest. Now you are not a mere bystander like the doctor or the soldier. Now, if you don't kill the patient you die. You are the captain of a military submarine travelling under an ice cap. The sub is severely damaged and you are running out of oxygen. One of the crew is mortally wounded and will die soon due to blood loss. There is only enough oxygen to get to the surface if you have one less crew member. Do you kill the injured sailor? Every single one of the empathy-impaired people said they would shoot him without hesitation. Sixty per cent of the rest of us would too. This time you are not doing the injured person a favour – rather, you are having to weigh up them living a little longer against everybody, including you, dying. Even so, 40 per cent of us would still rather die than have to kill the wounded sailor. To the empathy impaired, however, there is no doubt at all. When they weigh the value of their life against someone else's, there is no question to answer.

Most of the scenarios produced similar results. Whenever the empathy-impaired person was in danger, there was a huge gap between how many were prepared to act in the empathy-impaired group versus the control group. There was, however, one scenario where the control group almost gave the same answer as the empathy-impaired group.

Scenario 18 asks you to imagine you are the leader of an army that consists of warriors from two tribes, the Hill Tribe and the River Tribe. You belong to neither tribe. During the night, a Hill

Tribesman murders a River Tribesman. The River Tribe soldiers demand retribution, saying they will attack the Hill Tribe unless you kill a Hill Tribesman as compensation for the murder. The only way to avoid a war between the two tribes, one that will result in hundreds of deaths, is for you to kill a Hill Tribesman. Would you do it?

Like the submarine problem, 60 per cent of the control group would kill the Hill Tribesman to prevent the deaths of hundreds. The large number of potential deaths meant more people in the control group would act. But for the empathy impaired, this reduced the likelihood from 100 per cent in the submarine scenario to just 65 per cent. The personal interest trigger has been removed from the problem and so, once again, the empathy-impaired group gave the same answer as the rest of us. The only real difference, aside from the number of people in danger, is that you, the subject, would not be personally affected either way. Sure, hundreds of other people will die, but you will be fine, so normal thinking kicks in again for the empathy impaired.

How do psychopaths make decisions if their interests are not in play? They don't. They will usually delegate decisions about things that don't affect them directly. In the scenarios above, when the researchers forced them to make a decision they just gave their best guess at what most of us would decide. While you are struggling with the moral quandary in the trolley problem, they are thinking, 'I suppose most people would say saving one is the better option.' But they don't really care, and so in real life, they hand off decisions like that to others. If it doesn't directly affect the shepherd, let the sheep figure it out.

In Boddy's study of the psychopathic CEO, this type of behaviour was frequently mentioned. Managers reported that they struggled to get decisions on things that would have taken their previous CEO minutes to sort out. One manager said all she ever gets back 'is "just deal with it", no guidance, just deal with it'. This would result in decision bottlenecks, where the lower managers felt it was not within their power to make the decision and the CEO refused to do so promptly, or at all.

The authors of the study observed that the failure to make everyday decisions usually made by the CEO created an impression of leaderless-ness and a lack of vision that demotivated staff and devalued the business. When managers suggested decisions they would be met with, 'I am running the show, not you – I am the Chief Executive, not you.' This absence of direction from the top, combined with fear of being punished by the psychopath, led to a freeze in strategic decision-making in the psychopath's direct reports, which cascaded down through the organisation. The UK charity study painted an all-too-common picture of the paradox of a psychopathic leader. The psychopath simultaneously wanted to micromanage the daily decisions made by others, but refused to make strategic decisions unless their interests were directly affected.

Are psychopaths fearless? The answer is no, but it sometimes looks like they are. It is more accurate to say they are not fearful. When normal people were sitting in Robert Hare's lab watching the countdown to a nasty electric shock, it freaked them out. But the psychopaths remained cool. The shock hurt them just as much, and they were not fools, so why didn't it bother them? The answer is the mechanism for measuring risk is impaired by psychopathy.

6

In 2010, Kent Kiehl set out to precisely test whether psychopaths assess danger in the same way as the rest of us. He gathered together 67 male prisoners with similar IQs and assessed their level of psychopathy using Robert Hare's PCL test. There were 30 non-psychopaths and 37 psychopaths. He then sat them through a series of Wason selection tasks. These tasks, developed in the 1960s by British psychologist Peter Wason, simulate the kinds of conditional reasoning we execute when we encounter everyday hazards. Often a risk or hazard can be managed or reduced by taking precautions or changing our behaviour, and the Wason tasks are designed to test how likely we are to do that. The tasks are divided into social contracts ('If you take the benefit, then you must meet the requirement') and precautions ('If you engage in the hazardous activity, then you must take the precaution').

People doing a Wason test are told a social contract rule such as, 'If you borrow my car then you need to fill it with petrol.' The subjects are then presented with facts, for example:

Helen borrowed the car.
Dave did not borrow the car.
Brianne filled up the car with petrol.
Kirk did not fill up the car.

They are then asked whether they need more information to see if the person could have violated the rule. So they might say they know that Helen needs to fill the car with petrol because they know she borrowed the car. But they might say that they do need more information about Kirk, because all they know is that he didn't fill up the car. But did he even borrow it?

The test is to only seek more information if it is necessary. If you seek more information about Dave, then that is counted as a negative since Dave didn't borrow the car, which is all you need to know.

A similar task based on precaution would state the rule, 'If a person works with COVID patients, they must wear a mask.' The facts then might be:

Steve works with COVID patients.
Lisa doesn't work with COVID patients.
Phil wears a mask.
Alice doesn't wear a mask.

The Wason tasks test the subjects' ability to logically think through the impact of social contracts and precautions. As a control, a third type of task was included that used the same conditional logic but didn't contain a social contract or a precaution. An example of these purely descriptive statements was, 'If a person is from California, then that person will be a patient.'

Social contract	If a person borrows the car, they must fill it with petrol
Precaution	If a person works with COVID patients, they must wear a mask.
Descriptive (control)	If a person is from California, then that person will be a patient.

When Kiehl used the descriptive scenarios, there was no difference between the performance of psychopaths and non-psychopaths. They both performed badly at what were essentially straight logic questions with no emotional components. Both groups got the right answers only about 20 per cent of the time. This result was in line with other published studies done in the general population. We are all pretty awful at descriptive logic problems.

But when it came to the other two types of problem, the results changed dramatically. Non-psychopaths got social contract tasks right almost 70 per cent of the time and precautionary tasks right 75 per cent of the time. They were the same type of logic problem, but when they included a social or precautionary aspect, normal people got a lot better at figuring out the answer. Psychopaths also did better on these types of problems, but compared to non-psychopaths they were terrible at both. They got these types of questions right only a third of the time.

In other words, when a social contract or a risk was introduced into the scenario, non-psychopaths were twice as capable as psychopaths at getting the right answers. These sorts of logic tests show that it's not that psychopaths intentionally violate social contracts or take risks, it's that they can't take them into account in their reasoning.

Chainsaw Al Dunlap told Jon Ronson he saw this as an advantage. He was prepared to take risks no-one else would take. 'It's like *Star Trek*,' he said, 'you're going where no man has gone before.' Dunlap went on to observe, 'You cannot be a leader and cringe from evil and badness.' And he is right that this is often described, usually by people who write fawning biographies, as fearless leadership. But it is easy to confuse 'fearless' in the sense of 'courageous' with 'not fearful' in the sense of not properly assessing the risks. Psychopaths are the latter, not the former. They feel fear, but don't perceive danger, so the fear doesn't change their strategy. The psychopaths waiting for an electric shock in Hare's experiment were just as scared of what was coming as the non-psychopaths, they just didn't worry about it. It's not that psychopaths are courageous, it's just that they have an inability to assess risk and danger. This is why the threat of punishment has no deterrent effect on a psychopath. If they thought their plan was good before being threatened, they will still think it is good after being threatened. To a psychopath, all threats are empty threats, because they cannot assess the dangers in proceeding.

Donald Trump was the most litigious presidential nominee ever. Prior to taking office, he had been involved in more than 3500 cases – that's more than the next five most litigious US real estate magnates combined. Since leaving office, he has faced more lawsuits and investigations than any other former President. Trump has never been deterred by the kinds of legal action that might make other businessmen change their ways. And he firmly believes everyone else operates according to the same rules. As his aides told the *New York Times*, Trump once explained that threatening to sue is never enough. He said people ignore threats but when you sue them 'they settle. It's as easy as that.' Trump frequently boasted that he never settled, but an examination of court records reveals that is simply not true. It is, however, likely that Trump believes it. Psychopaths expunge failure from their memories.

Many of Al Dunlap's jobs ended in litigation with his former employer or shareholders, or both. Why didn't he change his ways? Because psychopaths believe themselves to be incapable of doing the wrong thing. If you are never wrong, you will never change. Failure teaches us to avoid repeating mistakes. When we hurt ourselves or others, von Economo neurons play an important part in engraving that lesson in our memory. If you don't possess that wiring, you cannot learn from failure. This is why psychopaths do so badly at tests like the Wisconsin Card Sorting Test, which ask them to adapt to changes in circumstances. They cannot acknowledge or learn from failure, so they always blame others for all that is wrong in their life and believe themselves to be infallible. When Trump began regularly losing lawsuits after becoming President, he blamed the courts. At one point after losing a case before the Ninth Circuit Court of Appeals, he demanded aides 'cancel' the court. He told them to draft a bill to 'get rid' of the judges. They ignored him.

Because they don't encode the previous bad outcome as something to learn from, psychopaths don't assess the danger like we do. They have no anxiety about the future because they cannot learn from the past. A normal person would not alter a map provided by the National Weather Service, understanding that if they were wrong and the storm did not in fact hit Alabama, they would be exposed as a fraud.

If you don't learn from failure, you are infallible. This is why a psychopath would alter the map. They are also not anxious about things that have not happened yet. They live in the moment and let tomorrow take care of itself. Even after the storm fails to hit Alabama, a psychopath would do exactly the same thing again the very next day, because they will blame the failure on anybody and anything except themselves. They are infallible, so their decision stands. To non-psychopaths this comes across as almost comical self-delusion, but a psychopath is not delusional, they simply lack the ability to learn from their mistakes. This is, of course, why psychopaths never show genuine remorse. How can you be remorseful if you don't accept you did anything wrong? If a psychopath appears to show remorse, they are lying.

7

On April Fool's Day in 1976, two college dropouts called Steve started a personal computer company in the garage of twenty-year-old Steve Jobs' family home. They named the company Apple because Jobs was a fruitarian who liked eating apples. Steve Wozniak was ten years older than Jobs and the only technical talent in the operation. Wozniak single-handedly designed and built the first Apple I kits. The kit cost $666.66, and required the buyer to build the computer from components sent by mail and supply their own keyboard and screen. Jobs called himself the CEO and took care of sales.

As another college dropout in Albuquerque called Bill Gates was discovering, the market for mail-order DIY computers was starting to take off. Apple made enough money in the first year to pay for development of the Apple II, a personal computer that came pre-assembled with a keyboard built into the case and a separate screen. It sold for $1298. Wozniak designed and built the prototypes, and a former Hewlett-Packard calculator designer worked on the exterior case, which Steve Jobs wanted as a differentiator. Jobs wanted the computer to look more like a kitchen appliance than a computer. He wanted the tech stuff hidden under a smooth appliance-like veneer, and he was heavily involved in the selection of the colour. But he went further than just choosing a colour. He was so unhappy with the thousands of existing shades of beige, he worked for months on a beige with a greenish tint which he registered as Apple Beige.

The Apple II was an instant hit, but not because it had a nice exterior case in a unique shade of beige. Wozniak had tapped into the start of the personal computing revolution. IBM could have built a better, cheaper machine with ease. It just didn't believe there was a market for it. The Apple II was expensive and not particularly capable compared to its Microsoft-based competitors, but it did allow users to create their own programs. One of those programs, VisiCalc, a precursor to spreadsheets like Microsoft Excel, drove enormous demand for the Apple II as a business tool. It flew off the shelves, with sales doubling every four months. By the time Apple went public in 1980, it had an annual revenue of $118 million, selling nothing but Apple IIs. But behind the scenes, the company was dysfunctional.

Like Al Dunlap, Jobs had an abusive management style. He would regularly tell Wozniak's engineers they were 'all shit', and would flit from division to division attacking and deriding most people in the company. He would regularly berate and belittle employees, and didn't seem to care about the damage he did to their egos or emotions. According to Jobs, this was intentional.

He later told his biographer, '[I]f something sucks, I tell people to their face . . . I know what I'm talking about and I usually turn out to be right.'

To defuse the situation, a new CEO, Michael Scott, was appointed to work with Jobs and moderate his management style. To keep Jobs from damaging the company further, he was assigned to oversee the development of the Apple Mac, a side project trying to produce a sub-$1000 computing appliance. The 'keep Jobs from meddling' strategy didn't work. In 1979, Jef Raskin, Apple's thirty-first employee and head of the Mac team, sent Mike Scott a memo listing Jobs' deficits. According to Raskin, Jobs interrupted and didn't listen, was irresponsible and inconsiderate, made absurd decisions, often personally attacked other employees, did not give credit where due, had bad judgement and was generally a dreadful manager. Referring to his dictatorial style, Raskin later told *Time* magazine Jobs would have 'made an excellent King of France'.

All of us are capable of being aggressively unpleasant towards people who upset us. Most of us moderate that behaviour using the feedback mechanisms that psychopaths are missing. Our aggressions are moderated by what scientists call 'distress cues'. When we see a person showing fear, pain or sadness in response to the way we are behaving, we change what we are doing. Those expressions are a sign of submission that evolution has trained our brain to respond to. It is a primal method of communication, one we learn before we learn to speak. When an eight-month-old baby sees a look of fear on their mother's face, they stop what they are doing. When they see a look of happiness, they keep going. This magic is performed by the almost psychic transmission of emotions that we call empathy. Psychopaths do not have empathy, do not feel our distress and do not respond to signs of fear or distress in others. The critical feedback mechanism is missing, so they just keep going where you or I would stop.

When our behaviour causes distress in others, empathy means we also feel distress. We encode a memory of that distress in much the same way we learn not to touch a hot stove. We learn not to do things that make others – and, via empathy, us – upset. Because the empathy wiring is missing in psychopaths, they cannot record those emotional impacts on others. Making another person sad or fearful is not recorded as a bad experience to be avoided. This means they will do exactly the same thing the next time, too – or worse. Our desire for personal gain is moderated by signs of emotional distress in others. Psychopaths are not affected by this. They will always pursue their interests, regardless of the cost to others.

Similarly, non-psychopaths generally avoid conflict. Past experience has taught us that conflict generates uncertainty and may be dangerous to us. Based on that experience, we will default to solutions that avoid conflict. Psychopaths are not affected by bad outcomes from previous conflicts. They are quite happy to enter into conflict with another person if doing so will get them what they want. Many people describe feeling like they have to walk on eggshells around a psychopath, because they are trying to avoid a conflict. But the psychopath has no such qualms.

We are all capable of anger. We get angry when we think we are threatened, when we expect a reward and don't get it, or when we think we are being treated unfairly. When something makes us angry, our amygdala sends a request for a retaliatory response, called anger, to our frontal cortex. We evaluate the likely responses of others and decide how or even if we will retaliate. We decide how angry to be. This all happens automatically, and so extraordinarily quickly we are not even consciously aware of it.

In non-psychopaths, the level of our retaliation decreases relative to the size of the likely response. At its most simple level, this is what is going on in Tit for Tat. We will retaliate, but only as much we need to. We will take an eye for an eye, but we will not take a leg for an eye. In psychopaths, this moderating mechanism is missing. Your potential response is not included in a psychopath's calculation. This is why you can't threaten a psychopath. They cannot evaluate responses that have not happened. This also means there is no brake on their anger. If you do something to make them angry, they will retaliate without regard to your response. You or I would pull back from an extreme and unrelenting response to a situation that made us angry. Our response would be proportionate – we would regard anything else as an overreaction, as vengefulness. But a psychopath lacks the wiring for moderation. When they are angry, they retaliate. And they do so without any limit imposed by your possible reaction.

Steve Jobs was a micromanager who involved himself in the minutiae of daily decisions. When he was frustrated by what he considered to be challenges to his authority, he reacted with anger. That anger was not moderated by the distress of others or by the potential cost to him in how others might react. Lee Holloway, the technical genius behind Cloudflare, changed from a helpful and nurturing leader and mentor into an aggressive and destructive boss on a hair trigger because Pick's disease had destroyed the parts of his brain responsible for empathy and self-control. According to Wozniak, Jobs was like that from the start. He said by the early 1980s Jobs was 'widely hated at Apple. Senior management had to endure his temper tantrums. He created resentment among employees by turning some into stars and insulting others, often reducing them to tears.' In later interviews he noted it was so bad that some of the most talented people at Apple said they would 'never, ever work for Steve Jobs again'.

Psychopaths value loyalty over competence. Their anger is directed towards those who frustrate their goals. Imagine you are a highly skilled and competent surgical nurse. You work for Dr Karen White, a renowned celebrity surgeon known for her groundbreaking work in the field of plastic surgery. One day, Dr White performed a complex surgical procedure on a high-profile patient. During the surgery, she decided to use a potentially life-threatening experimental technique that had not been approved by the hospital's ethics committee. Most of the surgical team complied with her instructions out of fear or loyalty, but you were not comfortable with her unethical approach. Discreetly, you voiced your concerns to Dr White, saying that the technique had not been properly vetted and could pose serious risks to the patient.

Dr White was frustrated with your refusal to comply, as she perceived your actions as a direct challenge to her authority. Unable to tolerate your perceived disloyalty, from them on Dr White began to undermine your work, spreading rumours about your incompetence and assigning you menial tasks far beneath your skill level. Despite your dedication to patient care and your expertise as a nurse, Dr White's relentless efforts to punish you for your lack of loyalty created a toxic work environment. Eventually, you decided to resign, unwilling to continue working under such hostile conditions. Dr White's obsession with loyalty and her inability to accept differing opinions not only destroyed her relationship with a talented team member, but also put patients' lives at risk.

Often the psychopath's goal is just to prove they are right, like Trump with the weather map or Jobs insisting on creating a particular shade of beige. But mostly their goal is to maximise benefit to themselves, no matter the impact on anyone else. Dr White wanted to be acknowledged as a groundbreaking leader by doing experimental surgery, and that was worth more to her than any risk to the patient's life. Trump valued the transient bump in popularity that pulling out of Syria would give him over the lives of thousands of allies, the resurgence of ISIS and the destruction of US power in the Middle East. When General Mattis questioned that decision, he was forced to leave. Psychopaths think of all other humans as livestock to be managed for their own personal benefit. The shepherd makes all the decisions. Good sheep go where they are pointed, while bad sheep react, and receive an angry response. Bad sheep need to be cut from the herd. If things go wrong, it is the fault of the bad sheep. If only they had done what the psychopath wanted, everything would have worked out.

Al Dunlap was mean, ill-tempered and arrogant. He would fire any manager that disagreed with his decisions and bring in good sheep from previous enterprises, who he knew would do as he asked. The UK charity boss forced those managers who showed independent spirit to leave and filled their places with 'yes' men and time servers. Often the 'bad' sheep leave of their own accord, as General Mattis did, refusing to bend to the wishes of the psychopath. But the result is always the same: the psychopath is surrounded by 'good sheep', people who will not challenge their decision-making. As one former National Security Council official said two years into Trump's presidency, 'I feel like you already don't have an A Team or B Team. You're really getting down to who's left that will say "yes."' The longer a psychopath stays in place, the less productive talent will remain in the team. Those who can leave do. Those who can't leave, stay, but they do only the minimum required to keep their jobs.

Are there consequences to the psychopath for the way they behave? Yes, eventually the community works together to eject them. But a psychopath will usually cause significant damage to the community before the consequences of their actions catch up with them. Unfortunately this can, and usually does, take years. People who discover the true nature of the psychopath usually quit, or hunker down to stay out of the line of fire. Often, organisations and individuals need to have suffered significant damage before it becomes clear there is a problem.

Holloway was not a psychopath, but his dementia had destroyed the parts of his brain that psychopaths lack in the first place. This made him act in the same way a psychopath would and, like Jobs, he was eventually ejected from the company he had helped create. Al Dunlap was eventually banned from corporate life altogether because he was unable to change his strategy. And Donald Trump was rejected by the electorate. Humans don't play 'be nice all the time', we play Tit for Tat. Eventually, unmoderated anger does have consequences, it's just that psychopaths can't see them coming. Like Dunlap, Jobs blamed everyone but himself. Psychopaths live in the moment, react in the moment, never learn from their mistakes and believe themselves to be infallible. According to the philosopher Carl Jung, the greatest risk to a warrior is misjudging the strength of the enemy. Psychopaths have no ability to judge likely retaliation and are not deterred by the threat of it. Apple had done everything it could to avoid firing its founder over many years, but eventually Jobs left them no choice, because he could not change his ways.

Aside from those of us regularly taking paracetamol, how many psychopaths are there? We can't be sure, but the research suggests the number is around 5 per cent of research populations. That means one in every twenty people you know is likely to be a psychopath. And the closer you are to the top of an organisation, the more likely you are to encounter them. The reality is that if you have a job, you are working with at least one psychopath. And unless you have adapted your behaviour to that reality, the experience is likely to be very unpleasant.

Next, I will introduce you to Jasmine, Alice, Scott and Stephanie. The characters and the story are fictional, but everything about them is realistic. Psychopathic behaviour is caused by a biochemical failure, and that failure usually plays out in the same way. So, while this is a work of fiction, as you read this, the scenarios illustrated are being played out in every workplace in the nation. You will recognise people you know in these characters, and one of them will be you.

5

Case study:
Stephanie

Stephanie had worked at the law firm all of her professional life. She had started as a clerk, working for a crotchety old litigation partner. The partner had been the principal lawyer for one of the country's biggest banks for much of the late twentieth century. Over her first few years working for that single major client, she had developed close relations with people at the bank, who would ultimately prove critical to Stephanie establishing her own banking law practice group within the firm and making it one of the pre-eminent groups in Sydney.

Her practice group had been growing rapidly in the last few years as she took on more and more of the bank's transactional work. Three years ago she had established a new team focused on mergers. One of her highly effective senior associates, Mark, would lead the team. The first recruit was Alice, a highly competent graduate. Alice's academic performance was impressive. During the interview, it became abundantly clear that, like Mark, she was a team player – someone focused on achieving the best possible outcome for the client, rather than grandstanding to advance her own profile. Stephanie also liked the fact that Alice's mother had attended her old high school.

Alice turned out to be a fantastic choice. She and Mark worked together brilliantly, and their results were so impressive that Stephanie successfully lobbied the partnership to award them both an additional bonus payment. She also decided to bring on two graduates in the following year. Once again, this proved to be an inspired move. The team worked together terrifically well under Mark's guidance, ably assisted by Alice. The four-lawyer team was a powerhouse, significantly outperforming both Stephanie's and the client's expectations.

1

The next year Stephanie decided to add another two graduates. One of them was Paul's son Scott. Paul was a senior partner at a rival firm. He was very well respected in the Australian legal community and Stephanie had a good working relationship with him. Scott was a university medallist and was just coming out of an associateship with a High Court judge. Stephanie was desperate to recruit Scott, and was overjoyed when she managed to get him on board. He would be an incredible addition to the team.

The other recruit was a less obvious choice. Jasmine did not have great marks, but she interviewed incredibly well. She knew exactly how Stephanie wanted the team to work and she was definitely a team player. She was driven and gung-ho, and in many ways reminded Stephanie of her younger self. Unlike many of the other graduates, Jasmine also had real-life experience working as a clerk in some of the major firms. She had also attended Stephanie's old school, and Stephanie thought she would be a good fit, given both her and Alice's connections with the old-girl community. It was not easy to convince her partners to choose Jasmine, but Stephanie staked her reputation on it, and in the end they relented.

Stephanie's choice was almost immediately vindicated. Mark reported that Jasmine was a pleasure to work with. He said she learned very quickly and was very good with the rest of the team. It wasn't long before Mark recommended that he delegate his duties around team management to Jasmine. Jasmine continued to impress, so Stephanie had little hesitation acceding to Mark's suggestion. This would also mean Mark could take on more of the client-facing work, giving Stephanie some much-needed help. Stephanie had noticed some of the team performance metrics beginning to slip since the start of the year. Billings were down, and non-billable time was increasing rapidly. She put this down to Mark being too busy to focus on running the team, and thought giving him this support was likely to turn the slide around.

2

Unfortunately, when the reports for the following month came in, it appeared things were getting worse, not better. Billings were still dropping, unbillable hours were still increasing, and sick leave was starting to grow well beyond anything Stephanie had seen in the team before. She had also heard rumours that many of the team had their CVs 'on the street', and word was getting around the firm that her team was not a place anyone who valued their career would work.

She asked Mark and Jasmine for an update. Jasmine explained that her new role had helped, but that Alice had become a problem that was disrupting the whole team. She said Alice had seemed upset by Jasmine's new role, and had become quite destructive to team morale. Mark confirmed he'd heard from various people that Alice had been bad-mouthing Jasmine. He said he had no specifics, but noted the increase in Alice's sick leave and said he had heard that it was 'mental health' related.

Stephanie was shocked. Alice had been with the team from the start and was an incredibly hard worker. She couldn't understand what could have brought about this sudden change. But Jasmine and Mark seemed convinced Alice was the source of the problem. Jasmine proposed some changes, including weekly team meetings, as a way of bringing Alice back into line and generally improving team performance. Mark and Stephanie agreed that sounded sensible. Unfortunately, over the following months, the problems seemed to get worse. Alice was clearly destroying the team's ability to function. Stephanie was frustrated and at her wit's end – and then the unthinkable happened.

*

3

Late one night Stephanie received an email from Jasmine containing evidence of a major ethical breach in the acquisition transaction that had been Stephanie's primary focus for months. One of Stephanie's clients was exploring a potential buyout of a smaller competitor. Both the client and the target were public companies, and both were clients of the firm. Stephanie's team was in charge of the work for the potential acquirer, and another team located in Melbourne were advising the potential target. The firm had invested significant resources in establishing confidential communications channels to avoid any possibility of a pre-emptive leak to the market or any exchange of information between the teams. Stephanie had just received an external valuation that suggested the target business was worth significantly more than the current offer. Mark and his team had been tasked with reviewing the valuation and checking each component against publicly available information before preparing a draft advice to the client.

Jasmine's email revealed that Alice had leaked the valuation to Chris, one of the lawyers acting for the counter-party. This was big, big trouble. Stephanie immediately advised the firm's indemnity insurers and alerted the rest of the partnership. Around 7 am she rang Mark at home and asked if there had been any important developments in the case. He hesitatingly said there was nothing to report. She asked him to come in early for a team briefing, saying she wasn't happy with the latest monthly reports and that she needed to sort the Alice issue out. He nervously responded that he'd be there in half an hour. Stephanie asked him to make sure Alice was there as well.

When Mark arrived at work he was called in to see Stephanie alone. She told him she was aware of Alice's email to Chris. She was shocked and dismayed that he had attempted to cover it up. She said there would be a disciplinary committee meeting in a few days' time, but that she thought it was unlikely he'd have a job at the end of the week. She then asked Alice to join them. Alice had no reasonable explanation for what had happened and was fired on the spot. Stephanie felt betrayed by both Mark and Alice. She had trusted them to create what had been a powerhouse team within the firm. She couldn't even look at their traitorous faces.

6

Case study: Alice

Alice had wanted to be a lawyer for as long as she could remember. Her favourite show during high school and at university had been *Suits,* and she pictured herself as the female version of Harvey Specter, the cool, suave senior partner who had worked his way up from the mail room to become the best litigator in the city. That dream had inspired her to put in the endless hours of study she needed to get the best possible university entry score and get into law at the University of Sydney. At uni she continued to excel, finishing her degree with first-class honours. When recruitment season came around she was one of the first students the national firms wanted to interview. She had her pick of offers, but decided to go with Stephanie's firm because she liked the quality of the clients she would be working with. It didn't hurt that Alice's mum had gone to the same private girls' school as Stephanie. Alice was one of five daughters, so as much as her parents would have liked her to attend her mum's alma mater, there was no way the family could afford it. Her mum hadn't been in the same year as Stephanie and didn't know her, but she remembered Stephanie's family and had nothing but good things to say about them.

Alice was to be part of a newly created team reporting to Stephanie. A senior associate, Mark, would be her supervisor and the plan was to recruit more lawyers to the team over the next few graduate intakes. But at the start it was just Mark and her. Mark was a very good lawyer and enormously supportive. Alice quickly found that while she excelled at the academic side of the law, she had no idea how to deal with the day-to-day processes involved in reviewing complex documents and providing detailed advice. But Mark knew his stuff, and carefully guided her through what she needed to do. When she made mistakes, Mark gave useful and constructive criticism. He always had plenty of time for her, no matter how much work he had on his own desk. She learned fast under Mark's tutelage, and by the end of her first year they were working together like a well-oiled machine. Stephanie was so impressed she arranged a bonus payment for the team.

The next year, Stephanie decided the team could be expanded more rapidly than originally planned. She hired another two high-performing graduates. Just as Alice had been a year earlier, they were a little rough to start with, but together Mark and Alice soon got them up to speed. Alice copied Mark's open-door policy and always made time to help the new graduates with any questions or feedback they needed. She only bothered Mark if it was something she had never seen before. Mark was getting busier and busier, but he still made time for all the members of his team. He trusted them to be the good lawyers they were, and to only come to him if they were unsure. The team felt supported and confident in their ability to produce high-quality work. By the end of Alice's second year at the firm, the team had again seriously outperformed all expectations. Once again, they all received bonuses, and Mark suggested that he was lobbying behind the scenes for Alice to be promoted to associate.

At the start of Alice's third year with the firm, two new graduates were added to the team. One of them, Jasmine, was an unusual choice. The firm usually only hired graduates with exceptional academic records, but Jasmine freely admitted that she hadn't even received second-class honours, though she claimed that was only because she couldn't be bothered conforming to the academic straitjacket the lecturers applied. Jasmine gave the impression she knew more about the law than any mere lecturer, but didn't want to waste her time proving it to people who didn't matter. She certainly didn't lack confidence in her abilities. Alice thought Jasmine's contempt for academic performance was an unusual attitude in a top national firm. But Stephanie had chosen her for some reason, and Alice trusted the senior partner's judgement.

Later, when Alice discovered Jasmine had gone to the same school as Stephanie, things made a little more sense. Although oddly, Alice's mum had never heard of Jasmine or her family. Alice tried looking at Jasmine's Facebook profile, but it showed nothing about where she had gone to school. In fact, it didn't contain much at all, just a glamourous photo of Jasmine in a ballgown. Her Instagram account was similarly barren, containing the same picture and nothing else. Alice's mum even dug through the school's old girls' database, but found nothing. The database wasn't created by the school; most former students voluntarily registered so they could maintain connections in the future. It seemed a little strange that Jasmine hadn't registered, but Alice thought nothing more of it.

The other new graduate was Scott. He had been a High Court Justice's associate and so was a year older than Jasmine. Scott was dux of the Sydney Uni Law School and a university medallist. Even though Jasmine and Scott had been at the same uni at about the same time, they didn't appear to know each other. But it is a big law school, thought Alice, and clearly they didn't have much in common academically. Alice's mum told her Scott's father was a senior partner at one of the firm's primary competitors, and his older brother was Senior Counsel at the New South Wales Bar. When Scott and Jasmine were introduced to the group, after suggesting high academic achievers were wasting their time, Jasmine had also said she wasn't a legacy kid, employed only because of who she was related to. Alice took this as a direct shot at her and Scott. If Scott noticed, he didn't show it, but it made Alice wonder what Jasmine knew about her.

1

Alice had problems with Jasmine from the start. Like all new graduates, she didn't know how to do the work, but she pushed back hard against any feedback Alice gave her, and would argue endlessly about points of law that were beyond doubt to everyone else in the team. She never did this when Mark was around. Sometimes Jasmine would make statements that were provably incorrect. If Alice followed up with her later and pointed out the error, Jasmine would insist she had never said it in the first place, often suggesting Alice was confusing her with someone else.

Alice found the constant point scoring tiring. Rather than get into another argument with Jasmine, she would frequently spend hours redoing Jasmine's work before sending it to Mark. She didn't have the time to do this, and couldn't put it on her timesheet, but as far as she could tell it was her only option. She didn't want the team to look bad, and the work needed to be done. Doing it herself was the path of least resistance. Thankfully Scott was no trouble at all, and Alice was soon able to trust him to produce high-quality work without the need for constant supervision.

Alice soon noticed that Jasmine was spending a lot of time in Mark's office. They seemed to get on very well, and Mark was obviously attracted to Jasmine, though Alice couldn't understand why. She wouldn't have described Jasmine as attractive and she certainly wasn't a patch on Mark's gorgeous wife. Even so, they seemed to be constantly laughing and chatting together. Alice knew Mark didn't have the time for this, but he always seemed to make time for Jasmine. It was a stark contrast to the way he increasingly treated Alice and the rest of the team.

Within a few months Mark announced that he needed to focus on client-facing work due to the significant increase in workload for the team. From now on, Jasmine would be handling any queries about administration, and would be responsible for reporting on the team's billing performance and liaising with HR and other admin departments. Jasmine would also distribute the work for the team and collate it for Mark's review. He, of course, would continue to be available for any legal questions, but suggested people talk to Alice or Jasmine before coming to him.

Mark was still happy to talk directly to Alice about the work and was still extraordinarily helpful, but he was pushed for time. His feedback became more brusque, and there was no extraneous conversation.

2

Jasmine immediately made it clear to the team that she should be consulted before anything went to Mark. She told them not to copy Mark in on emails because he needed to focus on the client-facing work. Alice would still occasionally talk to Mark about work, and even though he was always friendly and helpful, he made it clear he would prefer everything was dealt with through Jasmine.

Jasmine started distributing the work to the team. She said the instructions were coming from Mark, but they seemed to be both unnecessarily detailed and weirdly vague. Sometimes Jasmine would ask Alice to undertake a task for a transaction she knew absolutely nothing about. When Alice asked for more guidance, she would be dismissed with a wave of the hand and told to just figure it out – Jasmine didn't have time to do Alice's job as well as hers. When Alice did 'figure it out', Jasmine would usually respond that she had misinterpreted her instructions and ask for something entirely different. Alice wasn't sure, but she suspected that Mark was being told the work was late because Alice was unable to follow simple instructions.

Alice would receive detailed comments on her documents critiquing her writing style, grammar and even paragraphing. Jasmine said she had read once that there should never be less than two and never more than four sentences in a paragraph, and she was strangely obsessed with this metric. She would often go through 50-page legal documents and mark up every paragraph she deemed being of incorrect length. This was a huge waste of Alice's time, but Jasmine would insist the document needed to be redone, refusing to give it to Mark in such a state. Sometimes, Jasmine would circulate work done by the rest of the team but give Alice the credit, praising her in glowing terms without acknowlededging anyone else's contribution. Alice would try to speak up and give credit to the others, but Jasmine would dismiss or talk over her. The other team members said they knew Alice hadn't tried to take the credit, but the atmosphere in the office definitely grew less collegiate.

Jasmine made it clear that she did not trust Alice to do her job properly, and this started to erode her own confidence in her abilities. Alice found herself second-guessing her work, and she could see this was starting to affect the other team members in the same way. Everyone was now double or triple checking their work for fear of being pulled up by Jasmine. Alice tried talking to the other team members about this, but they would change the subject. She wasn't sure who she could trust. What if they told Jasmine that Alice was bitching about her? She was absolutely certain she couldn't trust Scott. At first he had seemed to be a valuable support, but he had started to withdraw into himself and refused to discuss anything, let alone Jasmine. Worse, he had taken to publicly complimenting Jasmine on her work. Alice knew it was precocious flattery, but Jasmine seemed to lap it up. Alice wasn't sure whether Scott really meant it or if he was just trying to stay on Jasmine's good side.

Jasmine was increasingly likely to pull Alice aside for a private chat. One on one, she would be vicious in her comments. She would tell her she was producing 'shit' work, saying if she didn't get her act together she would have to stop covering for her and let Mark know what was going on. When others were watching, however, she would joke and chat with Alice, just as she did with all the other members of the team. Alice had no idea whether Jasmine really was on good terms with the other team members or if this was just as much for show as her behaviour with Alice was. Alice began to dread giving any work to Jasmine, and felt under constant pressure. She knew Jasmine was a liar, but she wasn't confident Mark knew, or that he would support her if push came to shove. She also didn't feel she could talk to any of the other members of the team about it, worried they would report anything she said to Jasmine. She felt isolated and less and less able to cope with even the simplest tasks.

As her confidence seeped away, Alice found it was taking her longer to do the work. Add the constant revisions required by

Jasmine and she had to stay late every night just to tread water. The Monday meetings were already pointlessly wasteful, mostly because Jasmine spent large amounts of time telling lengthy stories, mostly bragging about herself. But the meetings also became a terrifying inquisition where Alice knew she would be called out yet again for failing to produce.

Jasmine began assigning the same task to multiple team members and getting them to compete to see who could do it the best according to her unknowable standards. Failing to be 'the best' would inevitably lead to some sort of public humiliation. This fight-for-your-job competition accelerated the destruction of any remaining trust between team members. In just six months, Alice's dream job had turned into an anxiety-inducing rollercoaster ride. She started to dread coming into work, and the mere sight of Jasmine made her stomach turn somersaults. Increasingly, particularly on Mondays, she couldn't manage it at all and would call in sick.

When Alice talked to her mum about what was going on, she was no help. Try as she might, Alice could not communicate why Jasmine's behaviour was so distressing. Her mum just couldn't seem to understand that it wasn't today's request to do a document that was traumatising, it was the cumulative effect of everything she did, combined with the overwhelming lack of trust in the team. Everyone was walking on eggshells around Jasmine. They couldn't trust each other, and increasingly, they couldn't trust their own skills.

*

3

One morning, after a particularly late night at the office, Alice was called into a meeting with Mark and Stephanie. Stephanie looked livid and Mark looked sick. Stephanie asked Alice if she knew Chris from the banking team, who had recently moved to Melbourne. Alice said she did. She and Chris used to have lunch together quite often before he moved, and they had kept in touch. Stephanie asked if Alice knew Chris was part of the counter-party team in the significant acquisition Alice's team was working on. Alice responded that she did. Stephanie then asked if Alice knew that meant there was to be absolutely no communication with Chris about the transaction. Alice said of course she did. Stephanie then showed Alice an email that appeared to have been sent from Alice's email address late last night. It enclosed a copy of a recent contentious valuation prepared for the acquiring bank and said 'Check this out!' Stephanie said Chris had immediately forwarded the email to Mark, together with a promise that he had not opened the attachment, but Stephanie said the damage was done.

Mark said nothing, and suddenly seemed to find the office carpet intensely interesting. By this time, Stephanie was so angry her face had gone a dangerously purple-red colour. She demanded to know what on earth Alice had been thinking. Alice said she hadn't sent the email, but could not explain how it had come from her account. She was fired on the spot. As she left the conference room, she noticed Jasmine with a smug, gloating look on her face. She didn't know how she had done it, but she knew Jasmine had sent the email. Alice had never hated anyone, but she viscerally hated Jasmine.

Alice walked out of the building crying uncontrollably, never to darken the doorstep of a legal office again. She would be the subject of an ongoing Law Institute investigation that would definitely end in her being stripped of the right to practise law, and might even result in prosecution. Her mental health, already precarious, declined rapidly. Within weeks she was diagnosed with PTSD and depression. Her confidence was shot, and even the thought of walking into a lawyer's office made her sick to the stomach.

7

Case study:
Scott

It sometimes seemed to Scott that he was related to half the lawyers in Sydney. Besides his father and older brother, two of his uncles, one sister-in-law and three cousins were in law. There was never any doubt that he would follow in the footsteps of his well-known relatives. So of course he studied law, and it turned out he was pretty damn good at it. His surname was well known in legal circles, and his graduation complete with university medal was eagerly anticipated by quite a few Justices who had their eye on him for an associateship. The most prestigious offer Scott received was with High Court Justice Phillipson. The work was interesting, and he loved being in the beating heart of the judiciary in Australia, but by the end of his one-year associateship Scott was well and truly ready to be a 'real lawyer'.

Once again he was flooded with offers from all the big firms. He flirted with the idea of working at his father's firm, but after discussing it, they both decided he should forge his own career path without whatever advantages, or disadvantages, nepotism might bring. He chose to work for Stephanie for two reasons. His dad could not sing her praises highly enough, and Scott loved the idea of being involved in some of the biggest financial transactions in the country.

On his first day he and the other new hire, Jasmine, were introduced to the team, who seemed to know and like each other a lot. The team leader Alice appeared competent and friendly. They all reported to Mark, who, while busy, seemed to be a very competent lawyer and good boss. Scott felt lucky to have landed in Mark's team. Jasmine had apparently also attended Sydney Uni, but he didn't recall seeing her before. She struck Scott as being an odd choice for the job. Her marks were only a little above average, which was strange in itself, but she also actively made fun of people who did well at university, which essentially meant everyone else in the firm.

Scott took an instant dislike to Jasmine but, as he told his dad later that evening, you didn't have to like everyone you worked with. His father agreed, but something else Scott reported did worry him. When Scott mentioned Jasmine's remark about legacy hires, his dad said this was a very odd thing to say, particularly when she knew Scott was related to some very influential lawyers. Scott thought his dad was making too big a deal of it, but Paul advised him to keep his guard up around Jasmine. Scott didn't know it at the time, but Paul also decided to see what he could find out about Jasmine.

Paul was worried because he'd had a very bad experience with someone like Jasmine before. Just after he was admitted as a lawyer, Paul had managed to join a small but prestigious firm in the city. The firm's partners included some high-profile senior lawyers, and Paul considered himself very lucky to have been accepted. Not long after starting there, he noticed that Richard, a junior partner with around ten years' experience, seemed to be targeting Lee, a junior lawyer, with innuendo about his competence. In team meetings he would exaggerate minor mistakes made by Lee. Richard also seemed to be spreading rumours about Lee's personal life, suggesting he was regularly seen with male prostitutes. Every chance he got, Richard would imply that Lee wasn't committed to the firm or the profession, and was really just a five-o'clock Charlie who was more interested in getting to the next party than producing quality work. From what Paul could see, none of this appeared to be true. In fact, it looked to Paul like Lee was one of the most talented and dedicated young lawyers the firm had. But Richard was relentless in his targeting of Lee.

Lee eventually left the firm and moved to London. Richard had also been spreading his lies among the profession in Sydney, so Lee found it impossible to secure a decent job in his home town. After Lee had left, Richard switched his attention to Cassandra, another very competent junior lawyer. She tried to bring the partners in to help her, but they sided with Richard and refused to believe anything she said. The partners eventually asked Cassandra to leave. Like Lee, she struggled to find a job in Sydney.

Then Richard started targeting Paul. Suddenly Paul was being accused of not following instructions when Richard had changed his mind about a task. Paul heard from the firm's secretaries that Richard had suggested he used his work computer to browse porn sites. And meetings were becoming a living hell, with Richard regularly conducting a Spanish Inquisition over imaginary errors Paul was supposed to have made. Lawyers that he'd previously had a good working relationship with were now actively avoiding him. There was something very odd about Richard, and Paul desperately needed to figure out how to defend himself against the bullying. Paul decided he needed to know what he was dealing with.

Paul started reading everything he could about workplace bullying, sociopaths, narcissists and psychopaths. The more he read, the more he was convinced that Richard was one of the people these books were describing. He began implementing the books' suggestions for defending himself while looking for a way out. None of it was easy. Every day he battled to convince himself to go to work. He spent all day on edge, not knowing when or where the next attack would come. Just walking into a meeting where Richard was present had begun to make him feel physically ill. But he survived it by taking thorough notes, verifying every task in writing and avoiding any discussion that was not entirely work-related. All the while he searched furiously for another job. Eventually he managed to find a lower paying job in a smaller, less prestigious firm, working for a partner who genuinely seemed focused on getting results for the client without destroying her team. It was a breath of fresh air, but it took Paul years to recover from his experience with Richard, if he ever really did. He remains vigilant for psychopaths and avoids interacting with them under any circumstances. Scott's stories about Jasmine were setting off alarms.

A week or so later Paul mentioned he'd run into Stephanie at a banking conference in Melbourne. After she'd finished telling him how impressed she was with Scott, Paul asked her what she knew about the other new hire in the team, Jasmine. Stephanie told him Jasmine had interviewed impressively. She seemed to know exactly what the firm needed and, Stephanie mentioned, she had attended the same private girls' school as Stephanie. It hadn't been easy to get Jasmine over the line with the other partners, Stephanie confided. They thought her academic record really wasn't up to the firm's standards, but Stephanie had pushed hard, and ultimately the partnership let her have her choice. Stephanie also asked whether Paul had heard of her, since she had done some clerking at his firm. Paul said he hadn't, but this was not a surprise. He did, however, ask which section she had worked in.

When Paul got back to the firm, he asked HR to search their records for Jasmine. They had no record of her ever working there. The firm's records weren't great when it came to casual clerks, but still, it was very odd. Paul warned Scott to be extra careful of Jasmine, and he regularly asked for reports on how she behaved at work. Again Scott thought his dad was overreacting, but he took his advice and remained wary around Jasmine.

Jasmine was difficult to work with. Scott and Jasmine would often be assigned to cooperate on the same piece of work.

Scott frequently found that he was doing most of the work while Jasmine spent large amounts of time flirting with Mark in his office. When she did put in any work, it was rarely helpful. She had a peculiar obsession about paragraph length and would occasionally want to insert large sections about legal cases or statutes with only tangential relevance, if any, to the work they needed to get done.

1

After a month in the job Jasmine and Scott were asked to do their first off-site. They were to report to the client's office and review a large box of documents that could not be allowed off the premises. They both arrived at around 9 am and got to work in the client's document room. It was dull work that required complete concentration. They needed to produce a report about the documents at the end of this engagement. On the first day, Jasmine told Scott she had arranged to meet a friend for lunch and she might be a bit late getting back.

She left at noon and didn't return until just after five. She told Scott that her friend had just broken up with her long-term boyfriend and needed a supportive shoulder to cry on. Scott said he understood, but her next request floored him. She said she planned to record her time as if she had returned at one and she needed him to verify her story. Scott was not about to lie for anyone, and certainly not Jasmine. He told her she could write whatever she liked on her timesheet but if he was asked about it he would tell the truth. Jasmine lied on her timesheet, but so far Scott has not been asked about it. Jasmine going missing for half the day meant once again Scott was left carrying the can. It was wearing thin.

When Scott told his father about the incident, Paul just said, 'Yep, sounds about right.' Perplexed, Scott asked what he meant. Paul said he suspected Jasmine of being a psychopath. Scott thought his dad had lost his marbles. Paul explained that he didn't mean she was an axe-murderer, although that was certainly possible. He meant she was a person who had absolutely no empathy. He explained that people with no empathy were compulsive liars who would try to manipulate every situation to their advantage, regardless of the cost to others. He said they are very dangerous people to be around, and highly destructive to any organisation unfortunate enough to have allowed one in the door.

Scott thought about reporting the timesheet issue to Mark, but his father advised against it for several reasons. Firstly, it is not his job to police other people's timesheets. Secondly, it was unclear how Mark would react. If Mark and Jasmine were as close as Scott suggested, that could backfire on Scott by making Mark an enemy within the firm. And lastly, if Jasmine is a psychopath and does get punished for lying, she will try to take revenge against Scott at every turn. Scott decided not to report it.

2

If Scott thought working with Jasmine was bad when she was a peer, it got immeasurably worse once Mark effectively put her in charge of the team. Now Jasmine was allocating and reporting on all their work. Paul told Scott he needed to start making a plan to get out of that section. Once again, Scott thought that was an overreaction, but Paul made some predictions about what would happen next.

Paul said Jasmine would start to intensely micromanage the team's work, that she would start spreading rumours about other team members, she would organise frequent opportunities to show that she was superior to them all, she would begin victimising individual team members in group meetings, she would take credit for work she hadn't done and barely produce anything herself, and she would blame others for any mistakes she made. Paul said this would destroy what little trust was left in the team. Productivity would go down, sick leave would increase and the team would slowly disintegrate.

As Paul predicted, Jasmine did start micromanaging and bullying the team. It was subtle, but it had the effect of seriously undermining Scott's confidence and his trust in the other team members. Jasmine's increasingly vague instructions meant he was now unsure if he was doing the right tasks. He also wasn't sure if Alice, who had previously been an enormous help, was part of the problem or part of the solution. She seemed to be taking credit for work that he had done. Jasmine grew increasingly critical of his work. He thought he had a pretty good grip on the law and how it applied to the transactions the firm was advising on, but now almost everything he did came back heavily marked up, meaning he often had to do the same work two or three times. He didn't know who he could trust in the team. They all came under fire from Jasmine in meetings from time to time, but it seemed to Scott that it happened to him much more frequently than it did to the others. On one occasion, after tearing him apart in public, Jasmine approached him as a 'friend' and warned him that Alice was threatened by his capabilities and he should be careful of her. Scott didn't entirely believe Jasmine, but it didn't make him feel any more at ease.

3

As each of Paul's predictions became reality, Scott grew more and more convinced Jasmine was indeed a psychopath. He knew he could leave, but jumping ship after such a short time in the firm would be hard to explain, and he knew it would be hard to convince other top-tier firms to take him outside of their annual recruitment cycle. They had all made their graduate decisions for the year. He also felt he was unlikely to get a good reference from Stephanie, and definitely not from Mark, if he bailed out when the team was already under so much pressure. Paul agreed with his reasoning, but said he needed to protect himself for as long as he stayed. None of Scott's dad's advice was easy to follow, but he tried as hard as he could.

The first thing Paul told him to do was make sure he had a written record of everything that happened. He suggested Scott email himself notes of conversations so there could be no dispute about when the note was taken. When Jasmine asked him to do something verbally, he should confirm the instruction in writing. Paul said this would avoid the increasing number of reworks he was being asked to do as a result of Jasmine giving vague or no instruction.

Scott began doing this the very next day. He was in the habit of eating lunch at his desk to try and keep up with his increasing workload. The rest of the team tended to eat in the lunch room or go out.

During lunch Jasmine came up to him, complimented him on his tie and asked him to work up an advice on the tax aspects of a new matter that had just come into the firm. He told her that he had very little experience with tax law and asked her to be more specific. She said she would get back to him. He knew what would really happen is that at next Monday's meeting he would be attacked for not having finished the work, even though she had given him no further detail. She would then assign the task to someone else, giving detailed instructions and demanding that it be urgently completed since Scott had wasted so much time.

After she left, he very politely emailed Jasmine and asked for detailed instructions on what was required. He said he would not be able to begin until he received the instructions. Later that afternoon, Jasmine forwarded an email from Mark which laid out the instructions in detail. Scott noticed that the email from Mark to Jasmine was more than a week old, and included a request that it be completed by tomorrow. It seemed to Scott that Jasmine was either incompetent or had purposely created a situation where Scott would look bad. Scott thanked Jasmine for the instructions and got on with the work.

From them on, Scott confirmed every instruction in writing and took detailed notes of every conversation he had with Jasmine. On his father's advice, he wrote up the notes on his own time, using his own personal computer. His father cautioned him not to let Jasmine know he was doing this. He said psychopaths are paranoid and sensitive to what they perceive to be criticism. If Jasmine found out he was keeping records of their interactions, she would likely react vengefully.

Scott emailed the notes from his personal email account to himself so that there could be no doubt as to when the note was made. His father worried that records could disappear from corporate systems, and said it would be hard to justify using the firm's equipment for this purpose anyway. He also advised Scott never to take his personal computer to work and to always ensure his work computer was locked when he wasn't in front of it, even for a second. He said too many corporate crimes are committed from unattended workstations, and that if Jasmine was indeed a psychopath, anything was possible.

4

Paul warned Scott that taking notes was by far the easiest thing he would need to do to survive the psychopath. The next thing he suggested would be hard to implement, because it felt so wrong for Scott, for the firm and for the clients, but Paul said he really had no choice.

Paul said Scott needed to be perceived as a loyal pet. There had to be no sign of resistance to Jasmine's whims. If she wanted four-sentence paragraphs, then give her four-sentence paragraphs. If she wanted full write-ups on irrelevant cases then that's what Scott needed to give her. If Jasmine said jump, his response had to be 'how high?' As long as the request was not illegal, he should do whatever Jasmine asked. Paul said this did not extend to doing anything that could put Scott in jeopardy, such as falsifying his timesheet, but Paul advised when requests like that came – and, he said, they would – Scott should politely decline without suggesting that Jasmine was doing anything wrong. Find a way to make it your fault, not hers, advised Paul. You can't do as they requested because of your strong religious faith, for example, not because they are doing something wrong. Always make it your fault. If you don't do something Jasmine has told you to do because you feel it is wrong, then when you are found out, it is always your fault. You are not clever enough, or didn't understand the instruction. The reason doesn't matter – the important thing is that it is never the psychopath's fault.

Paul said that Scott needed to master the fine art of being emotionless in the face of accusations or attack from Jasmine. He told him to always respond in a calm, unemotional way, to answer only the question she asks and never give additional information. Listen carefully to the question and make no assumptions about what is being asked. Do not fall for innuendo. A vague allegation needs to be nailed down. So for example, if Jasmine were to say she had concerns about his document, he should unemotionally ask what they are, not start trying to anticipate what she is concerned about and give her more ammunition. Most importantly, Scott should not give Jasmine any personal information and if he must talk about anything other than work, keep it bland and boring. He should be careful not to give her any information she could use against him or anyone else.

Paul said that in any sticky situation he should also try to distract Jasmine with flattery. He said psychopaths are highly susceptible to flattery, even when it is very obvious. Paul suggested complimenting her on some recent advice that she had prepared. Psychopaths believe they are the smartest person in any room, he explained. Try to do this in public whenever possible, he said. Paul also warned it was imperative to avoid embarrassing Jasmine. Never suggest that anything she does or says is not 100 per cent correct. If it is wrong, that is for someone else to point out, not Scott.

It was absolutely vital that Scott avoid challenging Jasmine in any way. This meant doing nothing that could be viewed as insubordination or as a criticism of her. Paul said psychopaths are no more sensitive to criticism than anybody else, but their lack of self-control meant that they would overreact. And worse, that overreaction would likely prompt them to seek revenge against the critic.

Paul emphasised that Scott needed to be very careful about this. He said a psychopath's paranoia meant that they were likely to take things that were only vaguely related to them as a direct personal attack. For example, if Scott were to compliment Alice on her contribution to something that Jasmine was claiming as her work, Jasmine would likely see that as Scott having a go at her. Needless to say, there is no such thing as constructive criticism of a psychopath. Avoid any criticism at all. Paul added that it is vitally important that Scott never say anything about Jasmine to anyone else at work. If even a whiff of negative gossip were to get back to Jasmine, it would likely stoke her paranoia even more and make him a target for her revenge. Paul forcefully reminded Scott that he did not want to be a target. This was a person who observed no moral limits in what she might do to exact revenge, and who had no real concern for the consequences, for her or the victim.

Paul said Scott should be very cautious about being seen with people who Jasmine regarded with suspicion, explaining that she would assume they were talking about her – after all, what else was worth talking about? Scott said this would make working in the team much harder, because who Jasmine disliked seemed to change on a daily basis. He said it would remove much of the informal collaboration that had previously made this such a well-oiled team. Paul counselled that it didn't matter. If Scott wanted to survive this, he needed to retreat into his shell, put everything in writing and do everything he could to avoid Jasmine's ire.

Paul acknowledged that having to walk on eggshells the entire time, being unable to trust his team, and constantly watching for signs of Jasmine's displeasure would make it nearly impossible for Scott to do his job effectively. But, said Paul, that was not Scott's problem. His job was to protect his mental health while planning an exit that didn't damage his career. Paul said the firm had placed him in this position, and they had to solve it.

When Scott wondered if he should go to Stephanie or HR, Paul asked if he was sure they wouldn't treat him as the problem. How did he know Jasmine hadn't been using her time to work them over just as thoroughly as she had Mark? Scott decided not to approach either, acknowledging there was a reasonable chance it could make things worse for him. Paul said the firm will either excise the psychopath or not. Either way, there was no point in Scott becoming collateral damage.

Nothing reinforced this advice more forcefully than when a few months later, Alice was dismissed for disclosing confidential information as part of a major acquisition. At first Scott didn't know whether Alice had done what she was accused of, but then he saw the self-satisfied look on Jasmine's face as Alice left in tears. He became laser-focused on surviving the remaining months of his graduate year and getting the hell out of the firm. He became even more determined a week later, when Mark was fired and Jasmine took over his job.

8

Case study: Jasmine

Jasmine remembers first noticing she didn't think the same as others when she was just four years old. Her mother regularly got together with her friends and their kids for play-dates at each other's houses. The kids would treat each other's houses as adventure playgrounds, and play relatively peacefully until their parents needed to leave to pick up older siblings from school.

Jasmine particularly remembers one of those endless playdates because it was the day Steven had been especially annoying. Steven was older than the rest of the kids, but not old enough to be at school yet. He had always behaved as if he was the commander of the kids, and regularly irritated Jasmine. He wasn't her boss, and she would only do what he said if she was planning to do it anyway.

One day the kids were at Steven's house, a fairly average Sydney suburban postwar bungalow with an extra-large backyard containing that most prized of playthings – a climbing gym set. This one was made from treated pine logs and had three levels, with a slippery slide from the second level. It was a castle. It was a steamship. It was an aeroplane. The kids loved it, and it would keep them occupied for hours.

Steven had decided that today the gym set was a pirate ship and he was the captain. He brusquely ordered the six or seven kids about, including Jasmine, and was generally at his bossy worst. An hour or so into the day, Steven and Jasmine were standing on the 'poop deck' – the third storey – of the incredible gym set, arguing. Jasmine had persistently refused to carry out his orders, so Steven had directed the other children to climb up and seize her in preparation for making her walk the plank – pushing her down the slide.

Jasmine was furious. Steven's orders didn't make sense, and who made him the boss anyway? She didn't even want to play pirates. She saw red, and in a split second decided Steven needed to shut up. The next thing she knew he was lying on the hard ground three metres below, screaming in pain. His left leg was at a very odd angle. At first the only sound was Steven's howls of pain, but soon all the other children were also crying, and some were running towards the house to fetch their parents.

Jasmine didn't know why the other kids were crying. She calmly climbed down to inspect Steven's leg. It really was at an odd angle, and was starting to bleed. It looked like she could see bone sticking through his flesh, but as she leant in to take a closer look she was interrupted by Steven's mum, also crying, pushing Jasmine away. Jasmine tried to show her the bone poking out, but she was too upset to pay any attention. Jasmine thought it was really very interesting. She'd never seen anyone's insides on the outside before.

Steven's mum had called an ambulance. Steven was still sobbing in pain, and the other kids still seemed quite upset. Jasmine wasn't sure why. None of them looked injured. But suddenly it seemed like Jasmine was being blamed for Steven's fall. Some of the other kids were saying she had pushed him. Mothers were intervening and Jasmine appeared to be on trial. She had, of course, pushed him. He was really irritating and he deserved it, but it was clear that was not going to go over well with the Spanish Inquisition forming around her, so she lied. She said Steven had grabbed her from behind to try to drag her down to the plank party. He had her in a tight bear hug, but she managed to slip free. In all the commotion he must have slipped and fallen. Jasmine watched the mothers' faces intently. Some seemed to buy it but others still seemed doubtful, so she turned on the tears and sheepishly added that Steven had been trying to touch her private parts. She said that it had happened a few times before, but she was too embarrassed to say anything. That seemed to do the trick. The doubters suddenly looked sympathetic, and any talk of punishing Jasmine was forgotten.

Steven's leg got better after a few months in plaster, but he was never included in the playdates again. Jasmine has no idea what went on between the adults, but she thought the 'fall' was a terrific turn of events. She no longer needed to put up with bossy old Steven.

Now she was the chief, and the other kids were very careful to do whatever she told them to. But that wasn't the memorable part of the day for Jasmine. She distinctly remembers feeling that she was missing something. When Steven was in pain, all the other kids and even the parents acted like they were in pain too. But Jasmine felt nothing, other than curiosity. She couldn't understand the big deal. Why were they all pretending to be hurt because Steven was hurt? She felt like something was going on that she did not understand and it unsettled her. Over the years since, she has noticed the same thing happening again and again.

1

In Grade 8, Jasmine's best friend Fiona was absent on the first day of school after the summer break. With tears streaming down her face, the teacher told the class that Fiona had drowned in the surf. She and her brothers had been fishing off the rocks with their father when a freak wave had washed them all into the sea. Her father had managed to get her brothers to shore but been unable to find Fiona. A few hours later, her body had washed ashore two kilometres away. It was a small school and most of the kids in Jasmine's class had known each other for years. Fiona's family had moved to the area just two years ago, but since the day Fiona joined the class, she and Jasmine had been inseparable. All the kids were in shock and many were in tears. Soon, the principal came into the room with a few of the parents. More and more parents slowly trickled in, collected their kids and left. They were all distraught.

Jasmine was shocked by the news, but it didn't upset her. It meant she and Fiona wouldn't be going ice-skating this weekend, and now she would need to find someone else to hang out with. It was hard to find people as loyal as Fiona had been. The search for a new best friend was not a prospect she looked forward to, since almost everybody else in the class seemed to dislike her for some reason. By now Jasmine knew that when everybody else appears to be emotional about something, it is best to act the same. So she turned on the waterworks and waited for her mum to come and collect her while trying to figure out who she could go skating with this weekend.

The whole school attended the funeral. Jasmine couldn't wait for it to be over. It wasn't just that it was boring, it was the emotional neediness that surrounded her. Everyone knew she and Fiona had been best friends and many people approached her, distraught and expecting an appropriate response. It was exhausting, and she was never quite sure she was portraying the right emotions.

The school arranged counselling for all the families in Fiona's class. At first Jasmine was curious as to what that might involve, but it didn't take long before she came to resent it. Her parents made her go to four sessions. They were all the same. The counsellor kept asking her about her feelings. She didn't have any, but he seemed determined to get something to write in his notebook, so she made up some stuff that sounded like what the other kids were saying. She had no clue whether that was what the counsellor wanted, but it seemed to end the need for sessions, which was a relief. Some of the other kids kept going to counselling for the whole term. Jasmine had no idea why.

2

Jasmine did well at school and got into law at university. By the end of her degree she'd been involved in three serious relationships and countless one-night stands. Jasmine thought of herself as slightly more attractive than average, and she never had any trouble attracting men or women if she got a chance to talk to them. She never really pursued relationships, just sort of fell into them. If she found someone attractive, she could do a nice line in charm that so far, no-one had been able to resist. It wasn't hard to do. She found most people like to talk about themselves, so she would just listen, then reflect back whatever she was hearing. If they liked surfing, she liked surfing. She would often back up that claim with a story from her past that would be almost impossible to verify. If they disliked a lecturer, she disliked them too. If they were overcoming anxiety and depression, so was she. It always amazed her how much people would tell a stranger if they were supportive and prepared to listen. She wasn't in the least bit interested in anything they had to say, she only did this as a means of deepening their attraction to her. She liked to move quickly to sex because that was the bit of a relationship she enjoyed most.

The problems arose when the other person inevitably became emotionally attached. They often mistook her apparent interest in them for some sort of emotional attachment. She liked them, and hanging around with them was fun, but she couldn't stand people needing her to respond to their emotional highs and lows. She didn't love them – whatever that was. She was there for fun, not to be weighed down by whatever they seemed to need from her. Jasmine would play along and try to act like she felt the same way but it was exhausting, and every now and then she just couldn't be bothered. That was always a mistake. Her push-back usually came across harsher than she intended and resulted in the other person being hurt, which required her to pretend to care even more. It wasn't fun, and seemed to make the neediness worse, not better. This often resulted in Jasmine trying to recapture the way she'd felt at the start, when they were strangers. She did this by sleeping with strangers. Inevitably, she would dump the partner trying to load her up with emotional baggage and move on. This often meant she would need to completely change social circles. There was no way she could remember all the lies she had told the last person and their friends.

Jasmine liked to think of relationships as being like a good bra. They were there to support you and make you look good. You might put some effort into repairing one if it started to fail, but after a certain point it's not worth the bother, so you throw it out and get another one. You certainly don't keep one if it starts to require constant adjustment. But if it does its job and doesn't require too much maintenance, you could keep it for years.

Her last relationship at uni was with Brad, a final year medical student. They were together barely two months, but Jasmine found his emotional attachment increasingly irritating. After one particularly annoying fight about 'feelings' she decided to sleep with his best friend, Alex. She had always sensed Alex was attracted to her but was barely able to admit it to himself. Alex initially resisted on the grounds of loyalty, but his chivalry was no match for the onslaught of Jasmine's charm offensive and a few too many drinks. She reassured Alex that it would be their secret.

The next day Jasmine feigned remorse and told Brad she had been drinking heavily after their last fight, had encountered Alex at the uni bar and one thing led to another. She had hoped this would be enough to make Brad leave her. Unfortunately it had the opposite effect. He was furious with Alex, and after a massive argument, swore never to speak to him again. Worse, it seemed to make him even more emotionally attached to Jasmine. He felt it was all Alex's fault and forgave her immediately. Jasmine didn't mind the make-up sex that followed, but Brad's need for emotional reassurance was really becoming a pain.

A week or two later, Jasmine overheard a conversation in the toilets at uni. Some girls outside her stall were gossiping about another girl's uncle being caught up in Operation Arkstone arrests. The Federal Police operation regularly arrested people suspected of being involved in the sexual exploitation of children. Jasmine's ears pricked up.

Jasmine had always found 'normal' sex a little boring and liked to explore some pretty out-there parts of the internet to satisfy her own interest. She regularly used Brad's computer to do this when he wasn't there, but she was always careful to make sure there were no traces of her browsing left behind. The next time she got on his computer, she decided she wouldn't be so careful. She visited some sites she knew had photos and movies of children, and she made sure the content was downloaded to

Brad's computer. To avoid it looking like a setup she deleted his entire browsing history to make it look like Brad had tried to cover his trail.

A few days later she anonymously reported Brad to the task-force. Nothing happened, so she did it again using a different phone and feigning a foreign accent. A search warrant was executed within days. Jasmine loved playing the horrified girl-friend. She never bothered to find out what happened to Brad, but she was pretty sure he never became a doctor.

Jasmine knew that people had a problem with being told lies. Frankly, she didn't understand it. She said whatever she needed to say to get what she wanted. People seemed to mostly accept her stories. Why did it matter if they were true? This is one of the reasons she didn't really use social media. She had accounts so she could research people, but she rarely posted anything herself, other than the most generic photos. Anything more than that just made it too easy to check if what she was saying was true.

3

Jasmine did well enough at uni to be considered for the graduate program of a large international law firm, but she was one of 83 applicants for ten positions, and definitely not in the top ten based on academic performance. She had noticed, however, that the interviewing partner, Stephanie, had attended an elite girls' school on Sydney's north shore. Jasmine modified her resume to list the same school as her high school, and also added in some completely fictional summer clerking experience at some of the firm's competitors in other cities. She figured she'd be able to charm her way past any questions about those. She also added that she had been accepted into a postgraduate program at Harvard and would need time off in six months to complete the residential program. None of this was true, but it sounded good.

Stephanie was about 25 years older than Jasmine and clearly tired of ploughing through graduate interviews. Jasmine dialled her charm up to eleven and used everything she had ever learned from flattering prospective sexual partners. She knew enough about the school to scoot through the reminiscence phase of the interview, helped in no small part by there being no overlap in the times they would have attended. And she knew enough about the competitors to give a convincing show of having worked there, however briefly. She came away from the interview certain Stephanie had taken a shine to her. And she was right. Within days the offer came to start in Stephanie's division.

Jasmine wasn't working directly for Stephanie. She reported to a senior associate, Mark, who worked for Stephanie. Stephanie looked after several large banking industry clients. The clients were a vital source of income to the firm, and Stephanie was a highly valued partner as a result. Mark was one of three senior associates who worked for her. Jasmine was one of five junior lawyers who worked for Mark and the newest addition to the team, along with another lawyer, Scott. Scott was a year older than her because he had spent the last year as an associate to High Court Justice Phillipson. Scott had attended Sydney Uni too, but they mixed in very different circles and Jasmine didn't know him other than by reputation. She knew that Scott had topped his year by a considerable margin. She decided the only way she would get ahead in the firm was to make sure Mark thought highly of her and less of the other four juniors. Mark's section was seriously understaffed. Mark was required to work directly with the clients and also supervise his team of five, as well as deal with any requests from Stephanie to help out the other senior associates. He regularly worked ten or twelve hour days and was in most weekends. His young family barely saw him.

The defacto team leader among the juniors was Alice. Alice was the most senior member of Mark's team. She had worked for Mark for two years before Jasmine arrived. Alice helped mentor Jasmine and Scott, teaching them how the team functioned and how to produce good quality research and advice for Mark. Initially, all their work was reviewed by Alice before she sent it on to Mark. Alice would frequently provide feedback and ask Scott and Jasmine to change or add things. Jasmine really objected to this. She knew what she was doing and felt Alice was just picking on her out of jealousy. She quickly discovered that if she argued with Alice over every little suggestion, Alice would eventually give up and do the work herself. Jasmine had no problem with this at all. It meant she could put very little effort into her work, get lots of free time and keep Alice out of her face. Of course, she still billed for the time the work should have taken, knowing Alice couldn't bill for all the extra work she was doing on Jasmine's documents. It was a terrific arrangement, and all she needed to do was occasionally give Alice a hard time over any suggestions she had.

Scott, on the other hand, seemed to knuckle down and do the work the way Alice suggested. What an idiot.

4

Over the course of the first few months, Jasmine gradually became a fixture in Mark's office. Thanks to Alice, she had lots of free time. She was a sympathetic ear and a quick learner. She swiftly became his work-wife, and he started to depend on her for advice. Although she worked hard to make sure Mark was attracted to her, she never let the relationship go beyond flirting. She knew flattering Mark's ego with the suggestion of attraction was all she needed to do. She made sure she also befriended Mark's wife to defuse any suspicions of the relationship. She found out important dates like anniversaries and birthdays and never let one pass without a gift 'from Mark' making its way home.

Jasmine slowly started to take over anything to do with running the team. She suggested Mark let her make decisions about workload and all the administration around task allocation and billing. Mark was grateful for the reduction in his workload and happily handed over most of his supervisory responsibilities to Jasmine, even though she was the youngest, least experienced member of his team. She even managed to cajole him into negotiating a small raise for her. Even better, he thought it was his idea. At first he occasionally checked on her work, but that became less and less frequent as he became increasingly involved in client-facing work, which he much preferred anyway.

When Jasmine asked Mark to direct the team to talk to her rather than bother him, he happily agreed. Jasmine was doing a terrific job of clearing his desk so he could focus on the work that really mattered. Now, the team that Mark had worked quite closely with barely saw him. They had to go to Jasmine with every question, and all their work passed through her hands first.

Despite being told that Mark needed to focus on the clients, Alice would occasionally talk directly to Mark about work the team was doing. Jasmine felt this undermined her authority, so she set to work white-anting Alice. Because all the team's work had to come through Jasmine, this was easy to do. On documents the team had worked on together, Jasmine would delete some of Alice's comments then paste them back in as her own. Sometimes she would change a case reference so that it was not relevant to the advice Alice was giving. And sometimes she would copy work from the other team members into documents produced by Alice, then circulate the work to Mark and the team, congratulating Alice on the excellent work. She also subtly let the other members of the team know that Alice was being paid much more than them. She had no idea whether that was true, but they seemed to readily believe it. When the inevitable friction developed among the team, Jasmine reassured Mark she had it under control while subtly suggesting Alice's 'personal life' was affecting her work. Once again, she had no idea what Alice's personal life was like, but Mark seemed to accept that vague suggestion as plausible, so she went with it.

Jasmine would often verbally assign tasks to Alice 'from Mark' that were slightly different to what Mark really needed. When Mark would express disappointment at the result, Jasmine would pass the feedback on to Alice and get her to redo the work. Alice would frequently protest that she had done exactly what had been asked. Jasmine, of course, denied ever asking her to do the wrong thing. On one occasion, Alice made such a fuss about it that Jasmine was forced to manufacture a fake email to Alice directing her to do what Mark really wanted. She showed it to Mark and he accepted it at face value, even when Alice later denied ever having received it.

Alice began to react aggressively to anything Jasmine asked, and started to complain to other members of the team about Jasmine's behaviour. Jasmine was always calm in the face of Alice's emotional outbursts, and feigned support with suggestions that perhaps Mark could lobby for more staff to take some of the pressure off Alice. She pointed out to Mark that Alice was taking a lot of sick leave, saying she had heard it might be mental health-related.

Jasmine was always careful to be charming with Alice whenever others, especially Mark, were around. When it was just the two of them, however, she would be very direct. She would tell Alice that Mark was worried about her attitude, and that she was also hearing complaints from the other team members. She would even occasionally suggest that Stephanie had heard rumours and was not pleased. It was all a lie, of course, but Alice seemed to believe it. Jasmine would go on to suggest that if Alice wasn't happy working for the firm then perhaps she should find another job.

The other members of the team seemed to respect Jasmine's authority. But she didn't trust them to do the work properly, so she always carefully checked what they did and would often send their work back to be redone because it wasn't how she would do it. She would frequently give the same task to a few members of the team and then decide who did it best. If they didn't do it well, she would talk through the mistakes they had made in front of other team members. She did this as a constant reminder that it was important to do things the way she wanted them done. The team didn't seem happy about any of this, but it wasn't her job to keep them happy. All that mattered was that they did what she said. And they did. The standout was Scott. He seemed to be the only one who really understood how truly skilled Jasmine was, and he often complimented her on her work. She was sure his loyalty could be depended on. She found she had to correct much less of his work as he came to understand the right way of drafting legal documents.

Even so, it was a big team and the others were nowhere near as reliable as Scott. Mark told Jasmine he had noticed the work coming from the team was dropping in both quality and turn-around time. He asked Jasmine if there was anything she could do about it. Jasmine suggested implementing weekly meetings to monitor progress on all the team's files. Mark thought that was a brilliant idea and asked her to action it immediately.

The meetings were scheduled for 8 am on a Monday morning, but Jasmine never arrived on time. She liked the thought of the rest of the team waiting for her to show up. It reminded them who was the boss. In the meetings she would ask each team member to report on what they had achieved in the preceding week. She would then allocate them further tasks for the coming week. She prided herself on being frank about their performance. If she thought their work was not up to scratch, she would say so. Sometimes the rest of the team would question the purpose of a task she had allocated. This infuriated Jasmine, and she would snap back that they weren't paid to question Mark's allocations; they were paid to do the work. That usually put an end to any discussion.

After being in the firm around nine months, Jasmine saw an opportunity to get rid of Alice. Mark's team was in charge of the work for the potential acquirer of a smaller company, and another team located in Melbourne were advising the potential target. All the team members had been thoroughly briefed on the importance of absolute confidentiality. Mark had been reviewing a new valuation of the target entity before preparing a draft advice to his team's client.

Jasmine knew that Alice was very good friends with Chris, one of the lawyers from the target's team in Melbourne. He had until very recently been based in Sydney. Alice and Chris often had lunch together, and rumours occasionally circulated that they were seeing each other. Mark knew this, and had asked Alice for her assurance that she would not speak to Chris at all about the deal. She had promised that would be the case. Jasmine had been present during this meeting.

Late one evening after the valuation work had been assigned to the team, Jasmine came back up to the work area to retrieve a document she had left behind. She noticed Alice had left her workstation unattended, and assumed Alice must be in the ladies room. No-one else was still in the group of open cubicles. Jasmine raced over to Alice's work station and quickly forwarded a copy of the new valuation to Chris with a brief cover email that said simply, 'Check this out!' She deleted the email from the sent items folder, grabbed the document she needed and left the building.

Later that night, a very flustered Mark rang her at home. He said Chris had forwarded him the email 'from Alice', together with a cover note saying it had not been read and his copy had been destroyed. He asked Jasmine what he should do. Should he report it to Stephanie, or should he destroy the email and deal directly with Alice tomorrow? Jasmine asked him to forward the email. After she had received it, Jasmine called him back and advised that it was probably best not to raise it with Stephanie. She reasoned no harm had been done, and he had previously assured Stephanie that he had explicitly dealt with Alice's relationship with Chris. Mark was hesitant – he knew the right thing to do was report it. But Jasmine convinced him not to, pointing out that if he did report it, then he would be admitting that he had not been supervising Alice properly despite his previous assurances to Stephanie. In the end he decided Jasmine was right. He deleted the email from Chris.

After she hung up, Jasmine forwarded Chris's email to Stephanie and told her that she felt it was her duty to let her know what had happened. She said Mark would undoubtedly tell her in the morning, but she felt it was important for Stephanie to know as soon as possible.

The next day when Jasmine arrived at work, Alice, Mark and Stephanie were in what looked like an intense meeting in one of the fishbowl conference rooms. Eventually Alice left the meeting in tears, threw her security pass on her desk and left the building.

Jasmine could see Stephanie's distraught face as she stood in the room alone after the meeting. I wonder what's like to be a partner, she thought.

Jasmine never saw Alice again, but she did hear later that she was no longer practising as a lawyer. Both clients commenced lawsuits against the firm, and Mark was also fired within the week. Given her experience in supervising the team, Stephanie asked Jasmine to act in Mark's role while she searched for a replacement. Jasmine's split-second brainwave had worked better than she could possibly have imagined. Not only was Alice history, but now she had a chance to work with Stephanie directly, and solidify her hold on Mark's job.

9

Psychopath wrangling

HOW TO DEAL WITH PSYCHOPATHS

Jasmine is not a strategist. She is situationally callous. When the mothers didn't buy her story about Steven falling, she distracted them with a horrific lie. When her boyfriend wouldn't take the hint and leave, she fabricated a sexual crime. When Alice stood between her and a promotion, she ended Alice's career.

The first important lesson to take away from this book is that psychopaths are not executing some grand strategy. They are simply living in the moment. They have no past and they're not worried about the future. Their lives are a minute-by-minute series of decisions about what is best for them, everybody else be damned. Donald Trump expressed it well when he said, 'Life is a series of battles ending in victory or defeat.' Notice there is no comma after the word battles. He didn't mean life ends in victory or defeat. He meant that each of those battles ends in victory or defeat.

Obviously, he would prefer victory, but if he loses, he moves on without a backward glance. This is why he claims never to have lost a lawsuit. He truly believes he never has. The losses are expunged from his memory because his lack of von Economo neurons means those memories cannot be recorded as a learning experience. This is why Lance Armstrong would do it all again, and I suspect if anyone asked Trump, he would too.

A psychopath's inability to learn from past behaviour means they aren't anxious about negative future outcomes. This is why psychopaths showed no anxiety about a countdown to a nasty electric shock. The non-psychopaths knew it was coming and became anxious. The psychopaths knew it was coming and yet were blissfully unconcerned. Their actions are not moulded by past mistakes nor by future consequences, for them or anyone else. Trump did not know he would be pulling troops out of Syria until he saw it as a way to calm Erdoğan down in the middle of a phone call. Jasmine did not know she was going to invent the molestation claim against Steven until the idea popped into her head as a way of deflecting blame for his fall. She did not know she would be claiming Brad had sexually exploited children until she heard the girls in the bathroom. She did not know she would be fabricating an email to end Alice's career until she found herself standing before an unlocked workstation.

The *Washington Post* fact-checking department has documented that Donald Trump told 30,573 lies during his four-year presidency. Some examples include the lies that he delivered the largest tax cuts in history, built the best economy in the history of the world, got more votes than any sitting President, appointed a record number of judges, and that Melania Trump was the most popular First Lady ever. None of these things were true. Frequently, the truth was the complete opposite of what he said. This is the second lesson from this book. Psychopaths lie *all the time*. Trump is by no means the first politician to be caught lying, but the sheer volume of his lies is extraordinary. And because he told these lies while occupying a position where every word he uttered publicly was recorded and fact-checked, the lies can be easily tabulated. But just because the *Washington Post* isn't fact-checking Jasmine doesn't mean she's not lying just as fluently – and not just about which school she went to or where she's worked.

It is not that psychopaths default to lies, it is simply that if a lie is more useful than the truth in a particular situation, they will lie. The result is an extraordinary volume of casual untruth. Some are big lies, some are small, but to a psychopath they are all necessary, even if only for an almost imperceptible gain. Most of us refrain from lying because our evolved Tit for Tat strategy means we expect to be punished if we do. We probably won't claim our wife was the most popular First Lady ever because we know anyone could easily disprove that claim. Just like the secretaries at Rand Corporation and the women who split the prize in 'KIIS the Cash', we worry about our reputation and refrain from cheating. We fear the consequences – whether we admit that to ourselves or not. We expect to be caught out in lies and we generally start from a position of telling the truth unless it is clear everyone else is lying. For the same reason, we also default to an assumption that the other person is telling the truth.

Psychopaths do not know shame. Normal people can be shamed into changing course. When Canadian Prime Minister Justin Trudeau was discovered to have worn black face make-up at a 2001 party, he apologised. He recognised that he had transgressed acceptable moral conduct and expressed shame for doing so. He agreed to abide by accepted social rules and conceded that this behaviour had not, thereby reinforcing those rules. But psychopaths don't worry about being caught, and catching them in a lie doesn't change that. When Donald Trump refused to apologise for his famous 'grab them by the pussy' comment, he showed that he could not be shamed into observing accepted moral behaviour, and in doing so gave licence to others to ignore the rules of social conduct.

Psychopaths are not playing Tit for Tat. They will say whatever gets them an immediate advantage and they have no concern for any potential consequences, including potential damage to their reputation. Those things are in the future and have no value to the psychopath when compared to the short-term gain of having people believe what they say at this moment. When Trump made the claim about Melania, she actually had the lowest popularity rating ever recorded for a First Lady, but the audience didn't know that for sure and his claim went unchallenged. Trump received the benefit of the false claim and let the consequences take care of themselves. Psychopaths suffer no indecision about whether to lie – it is as natural as breathing. We should always assume a psychopath is lying to us until proven otherwise, no matter how much we want to believe what they are saying.

The third important lesson is that psychopaths know absolutely no boundaries. Even if it occurred to us to fabricate Alice's email, we would immediately dismiss the idea as too extreme. We would worry about the effect such an act would have on her life.

We would worry about what would happen to us if we were caught. And we would not do it. Our brains are wired to take account of others in our decision-making, so even if we see short-cuts that benefit us, we moderate our actions with consideration for others. We worry about the consequences, not just for us, but for everyone else as well. All of this is completely invisible to a psychopath. To them, the world is a simple place where the only question they need to answer is 'What is the best outcome for me right here, right now?'

If you want to predict what a psychopath will do, then you must think like they do. This is not easy. You must remove any boundaries imposed by morals or concern for the welfare of your fellow human beings. You must also remove any fear about the potential consequences of your actions, for you or anyone else. If you get caught doing wrong, you'll cross that bridge when you come to it. Next, think of the options that benefit you the most. They don't need to be big benefits, just more beneficial than the other options. If someone would pay you a dollar to divert the trolley onto the track with five people rather than the track with one person, then that's what you'll do. This remains true even if the five people are your children. It is very, very hard for a person with working empathy to even imagine thinking this way. But if you want to know what the psychopath will do next, this is what you must do. Every time you find yourself thinking 'nah, they wouldn't go that far,' you need to stop, reframe and make sure you are not imposing empathetic limits. Yes, they really would get you fired so they could have your office, or even just your stapler. Yes, they really would blow up a valuable deal for your firm just because they didn't like a co-worker. No benefit is too small. No cost – to others – is too great.

The fourth lesson to take from this book is that psychopaths are masters of managing impressions. They have spent their whole lives hiding in plain sight. They know they do not react in the way communities expect, and they have continuously practised looking normal. This makes them experts at noticing what we want and, if it is worth it, giving it to us. Mark didn't know Jasmine was a psychopath until it was too late – and he may still not know what happened. Right up until the end, Jasmine was the perfect supportive employee as far as he was concerned. Stephanie still doesn't know, and won't know until Jasmine destroys her life too. Jasmine didn't bother managing impressions for the others in the team because they could not give her anything in return. She also ensured she was shielded from recriminations by the positive impressions she maintained with Mark and Stephanie. Had the other team members complained about Jasmine, they would have been met with disbelief, and probably accused of jealousy.

All of this makes a psychopath like Jasmine look evil, and by normal human standards she is. But she could never see it this way, any more than you could see yourself as evil for picking a flower. You like the flower, so you pick it. Who cares what the plant thinks?

The last lesson about psychopaths is that they will never change. They won't have an epiphany and discover that they have been evil. Psychopathy is a hard-wired condition that cannot be reversed. The kids at Mendota didn't stop being psychopaths. They were just trained, much like dogs seeking treats, to behave in a way that was more compatible with human society. And for a little while after the training, they committed less crime, but the longer they were away from that system, the less effect it had on their behaviour.

1

At least one in twenty people are psychopaths. Given that psychopaths are a reality in all of our lives, how do we behave around them? The answer is to think of them like a large and potentially dangerous pet – say, a Rottweiler. If you are the Rottweiler's master, train it well and control it. If you are anyone else, don't provoke it. Imagining your psychopathic boss or co-worker as a potentially dangerous, barely domesticated animal can be helpful when interacting with them. Think of them as a Rottweiler who is calm, but looking for any provocation to attack. You have wandered into a property being guarded by the Rottweiler and your job is to avoid provoking them while you calmly make your escape. This is an important lesson about working for psychopaths. The Rottweiler will never change its personality. Every second you spend in its presence is filled with the potential for danger. From the moment you know you are working for a psychopath, you need to be focused on getting away, just as you would if you found yourself in a yard with a dangerous dog. Obviously not being in the yard in the first place is the best possible option. But if you work with or for a psychopath, you are already in the yard. If you have a choice about whether or not to interact with the psychopath, then don't. If you can see the psychopath in the yard from the safety of the street, then keep on trucking. Do not enter the yard. If you can see that your boss is a psychopath before you take the job, find another job. The following rules are for people who are already trapped in the yard.

The first rule of interacting with a psychopath is: be a robot. Execute commands. Focus on remaining calm. Respond politely, but do not provide any additional information. This can be very hard. Psychopaths can be very charming, and when they want something from you they will use that charm to elicit information you might not otherwise share. Do not share personal information. If they start asking about your hobbies, partner, home or kids, for example, divert the conversation back to them, provide non-committal answers or bore them out of the conversation by banging on about your fictional love of trainspotting or your views on the intricacies of nineteenth-century African politics. The answer to the question, 'How's your wife going with her new job?' is 'She's doing well. Did you catch the Djokovic game on telly last night?' The psychopath should come out of the conversation with no more personal information about you than they had going in. You wouldn't tell the Rottweiler that the best place to bite you is on your Achilles tendon, so don't tell a psychopath either.

When you are asked about work, answer only the question asked, and do not respond to provocation. The answer to the question, 'Why didn't Leah get this done on time?' is 'I don't know.' It is not, 'Leah was having trouble at home.' This won't be easy, because unlike a Rottweiler, a psychopath will know how to push your emotional buttons. They know what things to mention to make you react emotionally. They might know, for example, that suggesting your work is sloppy upsets you because you take pride in how accurate your work is. The psychopath might know that you dislike a colleague, so will also pretend to dislike them to get you to gossip. They will, of course, pass anything you say on to that person. The possibilities are endless, and they will know and use them all, because if they can get you to respond emotionally they will know more about your weaknesses, and will be able to manipulate you more easily. When you feel the emotions rising, breathe, think, then respond calmly. The answer to, 'It's a pity your work was too sloppy to show to the CEO' is, 'Please show me areas where the work can be improved.' The answer to, 'Janice is bloody hopeless – I heard she was out drinking until 4am,' is, 'I don't know what you are talking about.' Do not say anything to the psychopath about anybody else unless you would be prepared to say it to them directly.

The second rule is related to the first. You are still a robot, but you calmly accept responsibility to avoid provocation. You do not bark back at the Rottweiler, you avoid giving it a reason to attack you further. The response to, 'You totally f***ed this up, you twit,' is not, 'Screw you, you gave me the wrong instructions.' It is, 'I misunderstood your instructions.' You then go on to ask them for precise instructions (which you confirm in writing) and tell them you will do it that way in future. This is unfair and will be hard for you, but this is about keeping you safe while you find a way to leave the Rottweiler's property. It is vital you remain calm throughout any interaction with the psychopath, no matter how much they try to provoke you. Like a Rottweiler, they will see anything other than compliance as a direct attack on them, and they will respond accordingly.

The third rule is to always have a pocket full of treats. No, do not throw doggy treats at your boss, but do have psychopath treats ready to go. Psychopaths value loyalty over competence and flattery over truth. If your psychopathic boss likes all work printed on single-sided paper rather than double-sided, then do it, no matter how stupid and wasteful you think it is. If your local Rottweiler wants you to spend a day changing the font of every fourth word in a document, then that's what you do. You will look at these idiosyncrasies and think they are wasteful and damaging to the mission of the company, but those are not your problems to solve. Your mission is to avoid being bitten by the psychopath while you make your escape. Once you know what the psychopath likes, give it to them, and add a little cream to the cake by telling them you think it's a good idea. They still won't trust you and they'll turn on you in a second, but you'll have survived another day.

The fourth rule should be obvious by now. Do not confront the psychopath. You may as well decide to wrestle the Rottweiler into submission. Perhaps you are tougher than the Rottweiler, but the dog is vicious and will not hold back or show any mercy. This is not a fight you can win. Remember, you are operating within the boundaries of morality. They are not. Confrontation will just get you gored. It will provoke the psychopath into considering you an enemy and they will use any means necessary to eliminate you. Obviously, complaining to the Rottweiler's owner is fraught with danger as well. If you go to HR or the psychopath's boss, there is a high probability you will be complaining to people who think the Rottweiler is the best thing since sliced bread. They will assume that you are the problem.

Scott had outside help who understood what he was dealing with. His father, Paul, took everything Scott said seriously and was able to provide day-to-day support in his battle to survive the psychopath. This is the critical fifth rule in dealing with a psychopath: we need outside support. We need to be able to tell our story and be believed. We need someone who knows the full story and who can help us work through the best strategy. Alice's mum was far more typical in her response. She dismissed Alice's concerns as trivial. This is a very normal response. Humans with empathy default to trust. We assume the best of people, and it takes a lot to make us change our mind. When you tell most people about the latest thing a psychopath has done to you, it will sound trivial. A psychopath asking you to print your report single-sided is trivial. Unless the person you tell knows, as you do, that this is part of a long, cumulative series of behaviours, they will think you are dramatising and ignore your concerns. If we are trapped in a yard with a Rottweiler, Alice's mum is the person passing by who points out that the dog is perfectly calm and asks what on earth we are worried about. Paul is the bloke who has seen lots of Rottweilers before, and who will hang around to give advice until we are safely out of danger. There are lots of people like Paul in our lives, they just usually don't run around telling us they have experience with psychopaths. When you come across someone like that, listen to what they say – it will be invaluable. When you find yourself trapped in a yard with a Rottweiler, keep your Paul on speed-dial until you are safely out of danger.

It is likely that your 'Paul' will be outside your organisation. Psychopaths work very hard to divide the flock. They will have many one-on-one conversations and will attempt to make each person compete with and distrust all other people. They value secrecy and centralisation of decision-making to them. They don't want anyone to have all the facts except them. This makes it much easier to manipulate people by lying, because it means nobody can readily verify anything they are being told. Psychopaths drain the trust from an organisation. They make us stop playing Tit for Tat and force us to play 'every man for himself.' As the old joke goes, survival is not about whether you can outrun a grizzly bear, it's about whether you can outrun your friends. This means that when a psychopath is in your workplace, you will never be sure who you can trust.

Scott didn't talk to his co-workers about Jasmine because he could no longer trust them. There is very little we can do to combat the destruction of trust, but we can protect ourselves against lies told about us. Like Scott, we must document every interaction with the psychopath and we must avoid all one-on-one meetings. We must confirm every instruction in writing in a matter-of-fact and unemotive way, and if possible, we must ensure other co-workers witness every interaction. None of this will mean we can trust our co-workers, but it will provide some level of protection if the psychopath comes after us. Think of documentation and visibility as a bite-guard to wear when confronting the Rottweiler. It won't stop the attack, but it will lessen your injuries.

How do we know Jasmine is a psychopath? If we are someone she no longer needs to impress, it will be obvious. If she is still pretending to be normal around us, it will be tougher, but there are telltale signs.

2

Alice may not have called Jasmine a psychopath, but she certainly knew she wasn't dealing with a normal person. She knew Jasmine was a manipulative liar and suspected she had a vendetta against her. She knew Jasmine was self-obsessed and callous. She knew Jasmine would take credit for the work of others and would blame others for anything that went wrong. Alice knew that Jasmine had destroyed the once-close working relationships she'd had with Mark and Stephanie, and she could feel the effect Jasmine's presence was having on the once-cooperative team, who were suddenly distrustful and competitive. Sick leave was through the roof, and she knew everyone was looking for other jobs.

Alice knew Jasmine didn't trust her to do her job, and she felt constantly micromanaged and under stress. The life and pleasure had been sucked out of her job, to the point where she dreaded walking into the building every morning. Her gut turned every time she saw Jasmine, and she just wanted to run away.

If someone around you makes you feel this way, they are a psychopath. Normal people can feel the empathy vacuum around psychopaths. We don't need to give them a PCL test or shove their head in an MRI scanner. They suck the life out of human interactions, making us feel alone when in every other part of our lives we feel like we are part of a group looking out for each other's best interests. One-on-one, a psychopath can keep up the charm well enough to fool most of us, but the mask will slip whenever a truly empathic response is required, or when they are trying to charm a group of people simultaneously. Your empathy subsystem will subconsciously notice these slips and you may feel perturbed by them. Do not dismiss that uneasiness – treat it as the red flag it is.

Alice's mistake was in underestimating Jasmine. She did not anticipate the lengths Jasmine would go to damage her, and couldn't even conceive that someone would destroy a valuable client relationship and wreck multiple careers just to remove a person she perceived as an obstacle. As a result, she did not take the precautions that Scott did.

Scott's precautions did not stop Jasmine being a psychopath. They did not remove her from his life, or stop her getting a promotion. Nothing Scott could have done would have achieved any of this. Deciding to take a psychopath on is roughly the equivalent of solving your Rottweiler problem by biting it. You might succeed if you are very, very lucky, but you are going up against a remorseless opponent who will fight to the death with no regard for the consequences. The sensible course is to keep the Rottweiler calm while you carefully back out of the yard. The only people who can fix the Rottweiler problem are the people who own the dog.

What if you do own the Rottweiler? How do you know, and what can you do about it? The view is different from above. Because psychopaths maintain their masks around those who can help them, they are almost impossible to detect unless you are deliberately looking for them. Until the end, Mark thought Alice was the problem and Jasmine was the solution. He was busy, and Jasmine was offering to take all the people-management off his plate. She was always helpful, and even his wife thought she was great. Stephanie had even less of a clue what the problem was. They thought they had a nice fluffy sheepdog who helped them manage the team. In fact, they had a Rottweiler who was savaging the team and would come after them next.

How could Mark and Stephanie have known they had a problem? The signs were there, but they needed to be looking for them. Sudden changes in sick leave rates, staff turnover and productivity should have all been red flags, no matter what story Jasmine was feeding them.

Once they noticed those symptoms, they needed to act. They needed to speak to all the team members separately, confidentially and without recrimination, and they needed to act on what they heard, even if it was the opposite of what they believed. Had they done this properly, they would have heard repeatedly that Jasmine was the source of the problem. While it might not have been clearly spelled out that way, each team member would have identified trust and micromanagement problems with Jasmine. Taking all these views together, Mark and Stephanie would have seen a picture of Jasmine that was diametrically opposed to the one they had. Mark would have found it especially hard to believe because he interacted with Jasmine day to day. Stephanie's distance would have made it more plausible to her. But they would still both struggle with the idea that their assessment of Jasmine was so completely wrong.

Why is it important that Jasmine be identified as a psychopath? Because if she is not detected, the damage she will cause will cascade until large parts, or indeed the whole, of the firm is destroyed. Al Dunlap left a trail of destruction behind him because he was not unmasked until after Sunbeam had been destroyed. And while each of his former employers realised what he was after it was too late, none of them were prepared to speak out and risk further attacks in the courts. It took a government regulator doing its job to finally end his career. The UK charity boss was not unmasked at all. The employee being interviewed in that study noted very early on, 'We are haemorrhaging staff . . . and it seems that every time somebody leaves, somebody with a particular skill set, be it web, be it data, be it creative, be it event organisation, whatever it might be, those creative people are being stifled and they are the ones . . . leaving.' By the end of the study the organisation had entered a downward spiral, with revenue plummeting and annual employee turnover sitting higher than 100 per cent. One manager had failed to get the board to dismiss the psychopath, and instead was summarily removed from the organisation himself. The psychopath sat comfortably on the bridge of his sinking ship, while the board assumed the crew were the problem.

It is critical that psychopaths be spotted early. The damage they do goes to the core of any enterprise. Businesses, charities, sporting clubs, political parties and most other groups exist as vehicles for cooperation. They are designed to deliver a common outcome which is greater than any one of us can achieve on our own. A psychopath destroys trust and teamwork, while stifling creativity and suppressing talent. When you employ a psychopath, you are asking a parasite to do something for the benefit of the host. The damage they cause is the result of the misalignment of personal and organisational purpose.

The effect is dramatic. People who can get jobs elsewhere, do. The organisation is left with a pool of workers who are phoning it in and staying out of the psychopath's gunsights. Needless to say, this has a dramatic effect on the organisation's income and every other measure of success. The firm loses all of the productivity advantages of cooperation, teamwork and innovation and, if it survives, becomes a second-class player in its industry. The longer the psychopath stays in place, the higher they will rise in the organisation and the more widespread their damage will become. And at all times, there is the risk of a catastrophic torpedo like the one Jasmine caused by inadvertently destroying a valuable client relationship and the reputation of the firm – all because she didn't like Alice. If that causes the destruction of the enterprise, the psychopath will simply flit to the next host, happily lying about the role they may have had in the destruction of their previous employer.

How do you protect an organisation from psychopaths? You design it from the ground up with honesty and transparency as core missions. Do that, and trust and cooperation will be built into the fabric of the organisation.

3

On New Year's Day in 1936, an American retailing legend was born into a working-class Catholic family in Pittsburgh, Pennsylvania.

But Jim Sinegal is not a legend because he co-founded what is now the fifth largest retailer in the world and the tenth largest US company. No, the former CEO of Costco is a retailing legend because he kept psychopaths out of his team, or at least made them play by his rules.

Sinegal didn't do well in high school, so Ivy League schools were not in his future. He completed a diploma at San Diego Junior College in 1955, then went on to San Diego State University to finish off an Arts degree while working part-time as a grocery bagger at Fedmart. Fedmart was a different type of retailer. Jim got a job at what was then Fedmart's only store. The company had been running its unusual retailing concept out of a 100,000 square foot former aircraft hangar in an industrial area of San Diego. It sold an eclectic mix of jewellery, furniture and alcohol on a near-cost basis. It wasn't really open to the public – in order to shop there you needed to be a member. The $2 lifetime membership was only open to Federal government employees and their families, as well as veterans and employees of the suppliers.

Fedmart had been created by local lawyer Sol Price, whose mother-in-law had left him the vacant warehouse. Babies weren't the only thing that boomed when the troops came home from the Second World War. There was also a boom in demand for retail goods. As a lawyer, Sol had been a strong advocate for the rights of the underprivileged. He started Fedmart partly because he wanted to undercut the big retailers, who he felt were using the high demand to gouge customers. Many manufacturers were exploiting laws that allowed them to set minimum prices for their goods. Items protected by this legislation were called 'Fair-trade goods', meaning they were fair to the manufacturer because they didn't need to compete on price. A fair-trade washing machine had to be sold for (say) $50, even if it only cost the manufacturer (say) $20 to produce. Sol thought he could cut the costs by creating a store that refused to stock Fair-trade goods and focused on the bare bones of retailing – eliminating advertising, cutting back on the range and extending the opening hours but implementing self-service. Self-service was a relatively new concept in retailing at the time. It was much more usual to hand your list to an employee, who would fetch your goods. Sol felt he could offer a much better price if he allowed the customer to serve themselves. His philosophy was to sell at the lowest possible mark-up rather than the biggest possible profit.

In its first year of operations, the store was successful beyond anyone's dreams, so Sol decided to add packaged food to the products on sale. This created the need for grocery baggers like nineteen-year-old Sinegal. Jim quickly discovered that he loved retailing and he really loved working for Sol Price. Sol's driving philosophy was that he owed a duty of care to his customers and members. They should be able to expect complete honesty at all times, and this extended to never making an unfair profit from them. This is why Fedmart never had sales. Sol later explained, 'We just always tried to carry honest merchandise at an honest price. I've always felt we had an obligation to our members to get them the best goods at the best price and not try to take an extra nickel out of them.' He had a similar attitude to his employees. He felt they should be the highest paid people in their community for the job they did, and they should be given the opportunity to invest in the company.

When it came to their beliefs about how to conduct business, Sol and Jim were peas in a pod. Much later, Jim credited Sol with teaching him the importance of establishing relationships with customers and employees based on trust. Working closely with Sol, Jim quickly rose through the ranks at Fedmart. He picked up his Arts degree in 1959, but by then it was clear he wouldn't be needing it. He was a low-cost retailer through and through.

The concept was incredibly successful. In 1968, Fedmart became a publicly listed company. By 1975, Price had opened 40 stores across the US with sales of $350 million. The success attracted the attention of other retailers, and later that year Hugo Mann acquired a controlling interest in Fedmart. Hugo was the successful founder of Wertkauf, a German chain of self-service grocery stores. Mann promptly fired Sol Price and started rapidly expanding the number of stores. In just the first year he added 30 stores. A year later, the company was losing money and within three years Mann was forced to shut down Fedmart.

Jim, who was by then the executive vice-president of merchandising, followed Price out the door in 1976 and joined him in his new venture, Price Club, an identical concept to Fedmart operated out of another aircraft hangar in San Diego. Sol made sure Price Club followed the same principles as the original Fedmart, and it was even more successful. By 1982, while the new Fedmart was closing the last of its stores, Price Club had established ten stores and was pulling in annual sales of $366 million.

The final demise of Fedmart in 1983 inspired Jim, who was then 47, to try his hand at running his own business. Sol wasn't happy to see him leave Price Club, but this was something Jim felt he was ready to take on. Partnering with local lawyer Jeff Brotman, Jim opened the first Costco warehouse in Seattle, Washington. When he started the company, Jim made three promises. First, he promised his customers they would never pay Costco more than a 15 per cent mark-up. Second, he promised his employees they would be treated with respect and would be paid a proper wage and benefits. And third, he promised his investors he would do his best to deliver a profit, but only after he had kept his first two promises. The investors need not have worried. Sinegal's venture was immediately successful. Costco opened three stores in the northwest in its first three months. The company went public just two years later, and was the first company ever to go from $0 to more than $3 billion in sales in less than six years.

In 1993, after refusing offers from Walmart, Sol Price – then aged 81 – sold the Price Club chain to Costco. The combined company operated in 206 locations and generated $16 billion in annual sales. Jim retired from Costco on his 76th birthday in 2012, leaving the job to his hand-picked successor, President and Chief Operating Officer, Craig Jelinek. Sinegal and Jelinek had worked together at Fedmart, so when Fedmart folded, Jelinek started as a warehouse manager at Costco. He rose through the ranks at Costco in much the same way Jim had with Fedmart and then Price Club. By the time Jim retired, Costco was selling almost $100 billion a year and making $1.7 billion in profit, yet Jim never took a salary that was more than twice that of his store managers. Today, Costco operates in 847 locations worldwide and produces a profit of $7.7 billion from $227 billion in sales.

Had you invested $1000 in Costco when it listed on the Stock Exchange in 1986, your shares would now be worth about $100,000. Costco has never recorded a year-on-year loss on a same-store basis. It is an incredibly solid, well-performing business. But many Wall Street analysts are not fans of the way Costco conducts its business. They think Costco is too generous to its staff. It has never laid anyone off, even during the worst economic downturns. The wages are relatively high, and Costco staff are covered by a generous health plan – an oddity in the US retail sector.

Wall Street also thinks Costco should be making more profit, but the company refuses to mark-up more than 14 per cent in a sector where mark-ups of over 30 per cent are common. Sinegal has always resisted calls to treat his staff like everyone else in the US retail sector. Jim feels that if you treat your employees well, they will treat you well. He says that the good employment conditions mean that Costco has extremely low rates of employee turnover and almost no theft by employees. Sinegal says that every level of the company should understand that 'honesty and doing the right thing' is just the way things are done around here. And everyone should be 'mortified if the company and its people don't do what they are supposed to do'.

Sinegal famously maintained an open-door policy. He made sure he visited every one of the company's locations every year and encouraged any employee to approach him with any problems they had. He also made this a rule for all managers. Costco employees knew their concerns would be acted on. Managers knew that if they didn't pay attention to employee concerns, they could well be hearing it from their superior. As Jim told *Ethix* magazine in 2003, 'If warehouse managers know that their own regional bosses have open-door policies and will talk to any employees about their issues, then they are going to be a little faster to talk to the troubled employees themselves. They don't want the problems to come back to them through their bosses.'

Sinegal also says this is part of the reason his customers are so loyal, with around 90 per cent renewing their paid membership every year. They know the low prices do not come at the workers' expense. Sinegal maintains this is not altruism, it's just good business.

Costco also treats its suppliers with respect. It doesn't negotiate special deals, it just asks that Costco be given no worse than the best price the supplier is prepared to offer anyone. In 2009, when Sinegal discovered Coca-Cola was offering a lower price to other retailers, he simply stopped ordering Coke. The company changed its pricing quickly and Sinegal put the product back on the shelves. This is as good an example of Tit for Tat in action as you are ever likely to see. Coke betrayed Sinegal's trust, so he retaliated, but as soon as they stopped cheating, he stopped retaliating – no hard feelings. Sinegal's entire business life appears to have been conducted according to the Golden Rule: he has always treated others as he would like to be treated. This is a stark contrast to the trail of corporate wreckage left behind by Chainsaw Al Dunlap. And it is a magnificent example of how to stop psychopaths wrecking your business.

Did Sinegal just get lucky? Was he in the right place at the right time? Do psychopaths not like working for big box retailers?

Or was his management style truly what psychopath-proofed his organisation? According to research published in 2015, the character of the CEO and the tone from the top really does make a significant difference to the financial performance of a company.

4

Dr Fred Kiel is a psychologist who has spent decades studying the traits and behaviours of successful leaders. In 2007, he and his team set out to interview 84 CEOs and 8500 randomly selected employees of US Fortune 500 companies, privately held firms and nonprofits. One of those companies was Costco.

The study involved asking the CEOs questions about the way they managed, and then asking similar questions of hundreds of their employees. The employees were asked questions like, Does the CEO 'own up to his own mistakes?' Does the CEO believe that 'people who make mistakes should be punished?' How often does the CEO lie to you?' And do you 'feel safe telling senior management the truth?' The study took over seven years, but ultimately provided the first hard evidence that when it comes to the bottom line, character matters. Kiel published the results in his book, *Return on Character*, where he introduces the concept of 'virtuoso CEOs', or leaders who possess a unique combination of character strengths.

According to Kiel, virtuoso CEOs possess four key character strengths: integrity, responsibility, forgiveness and compassion. These strengths not only help them navigate the challenges of leading a company, but also drive positive results for the organisation. At the other end of the scale were what Kiel described as self-focused CEOs, or psychopaths in the C-Suite (referring to the Chief Executive Officer, the Chief Financial Officer, etc).

Integrity is the foundation of a virtuoso CEO's leadership style. These leaders are transparent, honest and consistent in their actions and decisions. They understand that trust is the currency of leadership and they try to earn and maintain it at all times. Psychopathic leaders do not understand trust. They don't trust anyone and they don't believe anyone trusts them. They firmly believe that the only reason anyone does anything is out of naked self-interest. This is why Al Dunlap tied those leaders he didn't fire with the golden chains of overvalued options. He couldn't trust them.

Responsibility is another key trait of virtuoso CEOs. These leaders take ownership of their actions and decisions and are quick to admit and correct mistakes. They understand that taking responsibility is not only the right thing to do, but also helps to build credibility and trust with employees, suppliers and share-holders. The first step to learning from your mistakes is admitting you made them. Psychopaths can never take responsibility. They are incapable of believing they have done anything wrong. If you don't believe you have ever made a mistake it is very hard to learn from your mistakes. This is why psychopaths do so terribly at the Wisconsin Card Sorting Test. They cannot adjust their strategy to take account of new circumstances which are rendering their initial strategy ineffective.

Forgiveness and compassion are also important traits for virtuoso CEOs. These leaders understand that people make mistakes, and that forgiveness is a powerful tool for building trust and fostering a positive work environment. They are curious about others' mistakes, rather than blaming. They look for ways to learn from problems to build a better organisation, instead of persecuting people for making mistakes. They also possess a deep understanding of the needs and emotions of their employees, and show compassion and empathy in difficult situations. This does not mean they are big softies, just that their primary goal is improving the organisation rather than persecuting the individual. None of the players on Herb Brooks' hockey team thought he was soft, or even nice. But they all worked together as a team to prove to him that they could. He threatened to cut the captain not because he wasn't a good player, but because he was not playing for the team.

A psychopath cannot forgive others' mistakes, and would generally regard even trying to learn from them as a complete waste of time and effort. To a psychopath, other people's mistakes are only useful as potential leverage. Mark made a mistake in not reporting the email from Chris. Jasmine immediately used that to harm him. Alice made a mistake in leaving a logged-in workstation unattended and Jasmine immediately used that against her.

But what impact do these character strengths have on the bottom line? According to Kiel's research, virtuoso CEOs are able to drive significant financial performance improvements for their companies. He found that companies led by virtuoso CEOs earn up to five times the return on capital. They also record an average of 26 per cent higher employee engagement and much lower levels of corporate risk. The key reason for this is that virtuoso CEOs are able to create a culture of trust, integrity and accountability within their organisations. This culture not only drives employee engagement and loyalty, but also attracts and retains top talent.

5

When we form a group for a purpose, whether it be a sports team or a charity or a business, we are subsuming our individual needs to the goals of the organisation. When the aims of the organisation conflict with our personal interests, we choose those of the organisation or we leave. This is what Herb Brooks meant when he told the Miracle on Ice team that the name on the front of their shirt, 'USA', was more important than their name on the back. This is why Herb didn't want stars on his team. It's why he didn't want individuals to appear at press conferences. He wanted the emphasis to be on the team, not the individuals.

Psychopaths want the opposite. They want to be the star. They believe they are the only person who matters. This is often the first sign that you are dealing with a psychopath. They are late to meetings so everyone has to wait for them to make their entrance. They insist on flying first class when the company policy is to fly coach. They insist on having the corner office and the better parking space. They are better than the sheep and they want that recognised. When a manager doesn't behave this way, it is a good sign. When Kiel interviewed psychopath CEOs, it was often in grand offices with walls covered in pictures of themselves accepting awards and meeting famous people. When he met Jim Sinegal, his office was a standard-issue warehouse manager's set-up with a cheap desk and not a single picture of himself on the wall. Virtuoso CEOs subsume their interests to the greater good of the organisation. Psychopathic CEOs do the opposite.

When we form a group, we create policies and rules to ensure fairness. We try to preserve the 'Commons' – being what the organisation is created to deliver. We create employment policies and selection policies and sets of rules for how we will deliver on the organisation's purpose.

Psychopaths are incapable of acting as part of a team. They have a fundamental conflict of interest. Their interests are always more important than preserving the Commons. They will always go for immediate personal advantage over benefit to others. Our only protection against this is to enforce honest dealing. When Stephanie chose to ignore the firm's employment policy regarding academic performance, she was not dealing honestly. The firm enforced that rule for countless other applicants, but Stephanie, harried and sick of the process, made an exception because she wanted to believe the lie Jasmine told her about going to her old school. When Mark allowed Jasmine to subvert the chain of command and insert herself between him and a team that had done nothing but outperform, he failed to do his job with integrity because he wanted to believe Jasmine was his friend. When he allowed Jasmine to talk him out of reporting the ethical breach, he broke a rule he knew he shouldn't, because he was afraid he would look bad to his boss. The only thing that will stop Jasmine mortally damaging the firm is for every person in it to start acting with integrity and honesty, regardless of the cost. As easy as this sounds, it is rarely done.

No matter how much we think we cannot be duped, we can. I have lived among psychopaths. I have witnessed them devastate or severely damage lives for trivial gains. I have worked with people who were forensic in their ability to spot psychopaths in the workplace – except the one that worked directly for them and flattered them without mercy. I have had people I love tell me they were prepared to ignore red flags because they have neither the energy nor courage required to face up to the psychopath. We can all be deceived, and even when we aren't, we can be bullied into looking the other way. Psychopaths can so significantly intimidate us that we can choose to take the path of least resistance and accept their lies, even when every other person we know is screaming a warning in our face.

But I have also seen psychopaths controlled by groups that behave as cohesive communities. These psychopaths encounter individuals and systems that remain unmoved by threats or flattery, that understand the rules and refuse to break them, that set clear boundaries and hold fast to them, and that invariably adhere to the Golden Rule, regardless of any potential consequences. This is where psychopaths come unstuck.

Jim Sinegal is a virtuoso CEO because he lived by a code of honesty that was openly and clearly communicated. He always put the welfare of his employees before any potential profit, and they knew that. He felt that if he behaved honestly and expected others to as well, then employees, suppliers and customers would be loyal to his mission. This is a hostile environment for a psychopath.

There is no way to manipulate an honest person. A person with integrity who puts the interests of the business first will always check your resume. They will not allow you to subvert a co-worker like Alice, who has always been capable and competent. They will not be talked out of reporting an ethical breach.

Acting with integrity means doing so always, and doing so regardless of the cost. When Jim Sinegal dumped Coca-Cola he doubtless stood to lose a lot of money. But that was not factored into the decision. Tit for Tat requires retaliation for dishonesty and forgiveness for honesty. And that right there is the secret sauce to this book: always behave with integrity. Do not sacrifice your integrity when dealing with a psychopath, and do not continue to work for an organisation that lacks the integrity to deal with one.

Conclusion

On 15 July 1961, a 36-year-old soldier called Kijambiya passed his officer exams and was promoted to the rank of lieutenant in the King's African Rifles (KAR), a 30,000-strong regiment of the British Army used to police and defend the British colonies in Africa.

Kijambiya had been born in a minority tribal group at the fraying edges of the British Empire. His parents were members of the Kakwa ethnic group, a community spread across East-Central Africa. His father was an itinerant farm labourer who abandoned the family when Kijambiya was still an infant. Kijambiya's mother was a traditional herbalist and diviner, and after his father left, she moved her family back to her hometown. Kijambiya's education and career prospects were limited, and his formal education was minimal. When he was sixteen, he attended a local Islamic school, and though he might not have been educated or intelligent, he would eventually grow to be about 6'4" and was known for his athletic prowess. He left the school after two years with only a rudimentary education and drifted from one casual labouring job to another before being recruited to the KAR as an assistant cook in 1946. With persistence, determination, nagging and unyielding ambition, Kijambiya ascended through the enlisted ranks, becoming an Effendi Class 2 in 1959. This was the highest rank a black African could attain in the KAR at that time.

The late 1940s and 1950s had been a time of significant upheaval as many British African colonies moved towards independence. Kijambiya's unit saw action fighting against Somali rebels and was responsible for suppressing the Mau Mau uprising in Kenya. Kijambiya possessed a ruthless streak, unflinchingly enforcing the will of foreign powers against fellow Africans striving to break free from colonial rule. This quality was one his superiors valued. He never experienced any repercussions for the numerous accusations of murder, rape and torture against him. In fact, he was known for his extraordinary charm, a trait that often left a strong impression on those he interacted with.

Despite his extremely limited education and reputation for brutality, Kijambiya managed to become only the second African to ever pass the extraordinarily difficult KAR officer's exams. This was quite the achievement for a man who one contemporary officer described as 'bone from the neck up', who 'needed things explained in words of one letter'. The exact means by which he achieved this feat remains unclear, but it's highly likely he resorted to bribery, intimidation or both. It's also likely that Kijambiya benefited from the strong relationships he cultivated with British officers, who provided him with favourable references.

One of Kijambiya's first assignments as a newly minted KAR officer was Operation Utah in 1962, a mission to suppress cattle rustling by Kenya's Turkana nomads. After completing the operation, Kijambiya was accused of ordering the torture and murder of Turkana tribesmen. A Kenyan police investigation uncovered evidence of severe beatings and deaths among the tribesmen.

As a result of the investigation, there was a push for Kijambiya to face murder charges. But subsequent legal proceedings did not lead to any action against Kijambiya or his soldiers. His country's President was warned about Kijambiya, and was advised to consider at least dismissing him from the military. However, the President rejected the idea.

Following his country's declaration of independence from the United Kingdom, Kijambiya cultivated a close relationship with the President and climbed through the ranks swiftly, earning a promotion to captain and then to major in 1963. In 1964, he took on the role of deputy commander of the army, and a year later he was appointed as the commander of the army. Kijambiya's meteoric rise culminated in 1970 when he was appointed to the position of commander of all the armed forces.

But Kijambiya was an ambitious man and it wasn't long before he mobilised the armed forces against the President. Anticipating his arrest for misappropriation of army funds, Kijambiya staged a successful military coup on 25 January 1971, while the President was in Singapore for a Commonwealth summit.

After seizing power, Kijambiya initiated a purge of the army. The wave of violence extended to religious leaders, journalists, artists, bureaucrats, judges, lawyers, students, intellectuals, criminal suspects and even foreign nationals, with the Nile River often serving as a dumping ground for bodies. Throughout Kijambiya's eight-year reign, these killings – driven by ethnic, political and financial motives – continued unabated.

Kijambiya's rule was a disaster for his country. He was a ruthless and paranoid leader who was constantly suspicious of his opponents. He was responsible for the deaths of up to half a million people, including close friends and relatives, and for the almost total destruction of his country's economy. He was eventually overthrown in a coup in 1979.

Kijambiya means 'machete', and it was a nickname given to Ugandan dictator Idi Amin early in his military career due to the manner of execution he and his troops often used. After he seized power, he preferred to go by 'His Excellency, President for Life, Field Marshal Al Hadji Doctor Idi Amin Dada, VC, DSO, MC, Lord of All the Beasts of the Earth and Fishes of the Seas and Conqueror of the British Empire in Africa in General and Uganda in Particular'.

There is little doubt Idi Amin was a psychopath, and there is little doubt that many of the people who knew him, knew this. But he repeatedly managed to gain more and more power. The journey from assistant cook to commander of the armed forces is a very long one. At every promotion point, someone had decided Amin was a worthy candidate who exemplified the values of the British Army. At each step, someone had been charmed, threatened or nagged into rewarding a man whose solution to most problems was intimidation or violence. People who could have kept him from power repeatedly failed to do their jobs. Yes, he should have failed the 1961 officer exam, but there were many more hurdles that should have prevented him from getting even that far in the British Army. His role in the 1952 Mau Mau uprising should have been investigated and there should have been career-ending repercussions. He should have been punished for the 1962 Turkana suppression. But time and again, the gatekeepers failed.

When Jasmine didn't meet the firm's criteria for employment, Stephanie shouldn't have employed her. When Stephanie took the decision to the partners, they should have stopped her on that basis. Al Dunlap was repeatedly hired by firms that failed to do even the most basic check of his resume, the kind of check that would have resulted in immediate rejection. Processes and systems are a primary defence against employing and promoting psychopaths. Every time we bend them or shortcut them, we run the risk of allowing these people into our lives. There were undoubtedly political motivations for promoting a black African in the British military, but they should never have been a reason to ignore the processes that served the military well for centuries. We need to stick to the rules even if it means sometimes missing out on a potentially fabulous candidate. The more flexible we allow the rules to become, the more opportunities we create for psychopaths. Employing Idi Amin is never a good idea, no matter how charming he is.

Jim Sinegal built his business on the fundamental belief that he should maintain honesty, empathy and transparency, regardless of the cost. He pledged to be truthful with his staff and customers, to make a profit only if it could be accomplished without breaking these promises. The rules remained unbending, even when it meant that Costco could potentially lose money, shareholders or supporters. Jim Sinegal undoubtedly employed psychopaths. But he instilled a culture of honesty and transparency throughout the organisation, meaning it was impossible for their craven self-interest to damage the enterprise. A psychopath cannot last long in such an environment.

The fabulous thing is that most of us are wired to work that way, but the key is to ensure the leader is not a psychopath. Do that, and everything else follows. Identifying and actively managing psychopaths is not easy. Trained HR professionals fail repeatedly. But if the organisation is well run, there will be a built-in psychopath containment or expulsion function. If Jim Sinegal is your CEO, psychopaths will either leave your organisation or play by your rules. If Al Dunlap is your CEO, your company is spiralling towards annihilation.

Psychopaths are an avoidable reality in any human society. During 1954, Jane Murphy, a 25-year-old doctoral student, lived with and studied a group of 499 Yupik Inuits living on remote St Lawrence Island in the Bering Sea, between Alaska and the Soviet Union. She was there to learn about indigenous people's knowledge of mental illness. She also did cross-cultural comparison studies in Nigeria and Vietnam.

Murphy found that the isolated group had a word, *kunlangeta*, which means 'his mind knows what to do but he does not do it'. She found it was applied to a man who 'repeatedly lies and cheats and steals things and does not go hunting and, when the other men are out of the village, takes sexual advantage of many women – someone who does not pay attention to reprimands and who is always being brought to the elders for punishment'. Murphy also noted that the Yorubas, an African people from south-western Nigeria, have a word, *arankan*, which had a very similar meaning. It was not lost on Murphy that the description very closely matched the then relatively new use of the word psychopath, adopted by Cleckley in his 1941 book *The Mask of Sanity*.

When Murphy asked what Inuit would traditionally do about a *kunlangeta*, she was told 'somebody would have pushed him off the ice when nobody else was looking'. They were not joking.

In January 2022, Dominic Cummings, Boris Johnson's former top aide, provided a written submission to an inquiry into the PM's lockdown parties at Downing Street. In it he said, referring to Johnson, 'It's clear talking to people in No 10 and 70 Whitehall that many officials are desperate to shove the kunlangeta off the ice this week.'

Unfortunately, as much as it is a neat solution, we can't just push psychopaths off the ice. We have to be prepared to deal with them.

You may not be an HR manager. You may not be the CEO. Your responsibilities might be as simple as deciding whether you want one lump of sugar or two in your morning coffee. However, honesty begins with you. If you consistently maintain integrity, you'll be the least likely target for a psychopath and you'll avoid enabling their actions. It will sometimes be challenging. At times, it may seem like everyone else is benefiting from playing the psychopath's game while you're ignored, and that could be a reason to seek employment elsewhere. But it is not a reason to stop playing it straight. Transparent honesty and empathy are the only true defences against psychopathy. If you don't want to work with psychopaths, avoid working at any place where honesty and empathy are not the currency.

We underestimate the necessity for trust. We underestimate how much it is involved in our everyday interactions. We underestimate how vital it is for the operation of our businesses, our charities, our sports, our religions and our communities. Psychopaths destroy trust, and in doing so they damage, often beyond repair, the essential infrastructure of our society. But only if we let them.

We went to the bother of evolving powerful changes to our brains that allow us to not only preserve, but increase, the value of the commons. The only thing that can stop us doing that is allowing psychopaths to lead us or be part of our teams – so don't.

Acknowledgements

Nothing I write is a solo effort. When I started writing my first book, *Sweet Poison*, I proudly handed the first chapter to my wife Lizzie. She read it carefully then said, 'What on earth are you trying to say?' I explained it. She listened then said, 'Write that, the way you just said it.' I threw the chapter in the bin and started again. It was the start of our collaboration on everything I write.

Lizzie is one of the smartest people I know. She reads everything I write and gives me frank feedback about it long before my publisher, editors or readers get to see it. She also challenges the research I apply and the conclusions I come to. But she is much more than an editor and fact checker. Once she is satisfied that the research and my conclusions are solid, she implements what I suggest in everything our family does.

It is almost impossible to live free of seed oil and sugar in modern Australia unless you are as determined as Lizzie. It is impossible to avoid psychopathic personalities, but you are in a better place if you have a trusted and expert collaborator like Lizzie keeping an eye on your six. I just write about stuff. Lizzie implements it in real life. That is not to suggest we have succeeded in eliminating device addiction and its consequences, or in insulating ourselves and our kids against psychopaths; these remain continuing projects. But everything you read in this book, and all my books, continues to be road-tested in real life by Lizzie and our kids.

Ingrid Ohlsson took a punt on me and *Sweet Poison* when she was a commissioning editor at Lantern (Penguin). It was a very long shot for an imprint focused on glossy cookbooks, but she believed as passionately as I did that the world needed to understand how dangerous sugar was. I have written a lot of books since then and Ingrid has published every single one of them. She never tells me what she'd like to see me write next, but she has a sublime ability to pick through the random threads of things I am researching and suggest which might benefit from book-length focus. I wanted to write this book because I felt I needed to drill much deeper into the way psychopaths think, and why. Ingrid agreed and made it so.

Belinda Huang worked on *Brain Reset* and she's been running the show for this book as well. She maintains a cracking pace and makes sure the job of getting a book into a readable state never falls to the bottom of my 'do it later' list. Vanessa Lanaway did the copy edit and did a fantastic job of turning the vague semblance of English I handed over into fully formed prose with references that have been carefully fact-checked and scrutinised. What I write always feels less complete than what I had in my head, but together Vanessa, Belinda and Ingrid somehow got this book about as close to it as has ever been managed.

Another person who has been with me since before *Sweet Poison* is my 'agent' and friend, Frank Stranges. Frank is not a literary agent. His day job is doing mergers and acquisitions in the tech industry, but he believed so passionately in the message of *Sweet Poison* that he badgered Ingrid for a year before she agreed to read the unsolicited manuscript and meet me. Without Frank you would not be reading this book, or anything else I have written. So while I usually joke about him in my acknowledgements, he has been and continues to be an integral part of the team that puts my words in your hands.

Lastly, I want to thank a group of people who mostly can't be named for fear of reprisal. All of them have lived through close encounters with psychopaths. Some are still in their thrall. Most of them don't want to be named, but Paul Langenberg has allowed the curtain to be lifted. He informs the character of Paul, Scott's dad. The real Paul is not a lawyer but he is a wise head who has earned his stripes dealing with real life psychopaths. The reality testing he and many unnamed others provided was invaluable.

Endnotes

1 Chameleons among us

p. 7 Richardson declined, citing . . .: O'Connor PC, 'A Taranto-Pearl Harbor Connection', *U.S. Naval Institute*, 2016, www.usni.org/magazines/naval-history-magazine/2016/december/taranto-pearl-harbor-connection

p. 7 The Abwehr had provided Popov . . .: Koster J, 'Dusko Popov: The Triple-Agent, Real-Life James Bond Who Warned the U.S. About Pearl Harbor', *History on the Net*, www.historyonthenet.com/dusko-popov-the-triple-agent-real-life-james-bond-who-warned-the-u-s-about-pearl-harbor

p. 9 The report concluded that . . .: U.S. Anti-Doping Agency, *Report on Proceedings: United States Anti-Doping Agency v Lance Armstrong*, 2012, www.usada.org/athletes/results/u-s-postal-service-pro-cycling-team-investigation

p. 9 When the team masseuse, Emma Reilly . . .: Fotheringham W, 'Emma O'Reilly: "My Relationship with Lance Armstrong was and still is a human one", *Guardian*, 2014, www.theguardian.com/sport/2014/jul/02/emma-o-reilly-lance-armstrong-cyclist-doping

p. 10 When Hamilton became a witness . . .: Macur J, 'Armstrong Encounter Draws Scrutiny by F.B.I.', 2011, *New York Times*, www.nytimes.com/2011/06/15/sports/cycling/altercation-between-lance-armstrong-and-tyler-hamilton-interests-fbi; Saletan W, 'One Big Lie', *Slate*, 2013, slate.com/news-and-politics/2013/01/lance-armstrongs-oprah-interview-his-threats-and-bullying-are-the-real-story

p. 10 When Winfrey raised his long history . . .: 'Lance Armstrong's Confession', YouTube, *Oprah Winfrey Network*, 17 January 2013, www.youtube.com/watch?v=N_0PSZ59Aws

p. 10 In a 2015 BBC interview . . .: Roan D, 'Lance Armstrong on drugs, history and the future', *BBC*, 2015, www.bbc.com/sport/av/cycling/30984312

p. 12 In high-trust organisations, employees . . .: Feintzeig R, 'Flexibility at Work: Worth Skipping a Raise?', *Wall Street Journal*, 2014, www.wsj.com/articles/BL-ATWORKB-2141

p. 13 As one of his aides once said . . .: Kutler S, 'Hoover's Abuse of Power', *Chicago Tribune*, 1991, www.chicagotribune.com/news/ct-xpm-1991-09-08-9103070622-story

p. 13 He famously had a file . . .: Talbot M, 'J. Edgar Hoover, Public Enemy No. 1', *New Yorker*, 2022, www.newyorker.com/magazine/2022/11/21/j-edgar-hoover-public-enemy-no-1

p. 13 Even John F Kennedy, who hated . . .: Guariglia M, 'What Happened Between John F. Kennedy and J. Edgar Hoover?', *Visions of Red*, 2012, blogs.dickinson.edu/hist-fbi

p. 13 When Richard Nixon tried to . . .: Talbot M, 'J. Edgar Hoover, Public Enemy No. 1', *New Yorker*, 2022, www.newyorker.com/magazine/2022/11/21/j-edgar-hoover-public-enemy-no-1

p. 14 In a 2020 ESPN documentary . . .: Zenovich M (dir.), *Lance: Part 1 (ESPN 30 for 30)*, 2020, www.espn.com.au/olympics/story/_/id/29209116/lance-part-1-how-watch-stream-espn-lance-armstrong-documentary

2 The evolution of empathy

p. 22 Brooks didn't want 'the ignorant . . .: Swift EM, 'A Reminder of What We Can Be', *Sports Illustrated*, 1980, vault.si.com/vault/1980/12/22/a-reminder-of-what-we-can-be

p. 22 A famous scene from the 1981 movie . . .: O'Connor G (dir.), 'Miracle – The Name on the Front More Important than the

Name on the Back', video, *Miracle*, YouTube, 2004 (uploaded 24 February 2012), www.youtube.com/watch?v=2nR3reKPE5Y

p. 22   By all accounts, the scene . . .: Mitzutani D, '"Again!" An oral history of Herb Brooks'(in)famous bag skate in Norway', *Pioneer Press*, 2020, www.twincities.com/2020/02/20/again-an-oral-history-of-the-infamous-herb-brooks-bag-skate-in-norway

p. 24   Brooks later attributed their frequent . . .: 'About Coach Brooks', *Herb Brooks Foundation*, www.herbbrooksfoundation.com/coachbrooks

p. 25   As *Sports Illustrated* writer Ed Swift wrote . . .: Swift EM, 'A Reminder of What We Can Be', *Sports Illustrated*, 1980, vault.si.com/vault/1980/12/22/a-reminder-of-what-we-can-be

p. 27   Marbury later described the Olympic . . .: Matthew W, 'Stephon Marbury Calls 2004 Olympics Experience the "Worst 38 Days of My Life"', *Complex*, 2017, www.complex.com/sports/2017/07/stephon-marbury-calls-2004-olympics-experience-worst-38-days-of-my-life

p. 27   When Argentina crushed the US team's chance . . .: Helin K, 'Remembering what went wrong in 2000-2004 Olympics for Team USA', *NBC Sports*, 2016, nba.nbcsports.com/2016/08/02/remembering-what-went-wrong-in-2000-2004-olympics-for-team-usa

p. 29   As Mark Pavelich, the player . . .: Swift EM, 'A Reminder of What We Can Be', *Sports Illustrated*, 1980, vault.si.com/vault/1980/12/22/a-reminder-of-what-we-can-be

p. 30   In 2006, Robert Huckman and Gary Pisano . . .: Huckman RS, Pisano GP, 'The Firm Specificity of Individual Performance: Evidence from Cardiac Surgery', *Management Science*, vol. 52, no. 4, p. 473–88, 2006, doi.org/10.1287/mnsc.1050.0464

p. 30   Robert Huckman later went on to look at . . .: Huckman RS, Staats BR & Upton DM, 'Team Familiarity, Role Experience, and Performance: Evidence from Indian Software Services', *Management Science*, vol. 55, no. 1, p. 85–100, 2009, doi.org/10.1109/EMR.2012.6172773

p. 33   The researchers tested this theory in the real world . . .: Flood MM, 'Some Experimental Games', *U.S. Air Force Project Rand*, 1952, www.rand.org/content/dam/rand/pubs/research_memoranda/2008/RM789-1.pdf

p. 35　In the early 1980s, Robert Axelrod . . .: Axelrod R, *The Evolution of Cooperation: The Revised Edition*, 2009, Basic Books, New York

p. 37　If you want to see this played out visually . . .: Case N, 'The Evolution of Trust', *NCase*, 2017, ncase.me/trust

p. 37　Mirroring behaviour is part of almost every . . .: The Golden Rule Project (www.goldenruleproject.org/formulations) is a great resource that collects together all the known formulations of the Golden Rule.

p. 38　Old Testament books tell us to take . . .: 'Exodus 21:23-27', *The New King James Bible*, biblia.com/books/nkjv/Ex21.23

p. 38　This was an expression of the foundational Roman legal principle . . .: Which was derived from the Code of Hammurabi, the first written legal system created by the Babylonian civilisation in about 1750 BCE.

p. 38　You don't kill the man and hold a grudge . . .: 'Leviticus 19:18', *The New King James Bible*, biblia.com/bible/nkjv/Le19.18

p. 40　Mirror neurons were first discovered . . .: Pellegrino G, Fadiga L, 'Understanding motor events: a neurophysiological study', *Experimental Brain Research*, vol. 91, p. 176–80, 2004, link.springer.com/article/10.1007/BF00230027

p. 41　Rizzolatti followed up this research with . . .: Iacoboni M et al., 'Cortical mechanisms of human imitation', *Science*, vol. 286, no. 5449, p. 2526–8, 1999, pubmed.ncbi.nlm.nih.gov/10617472

p. 42　This was put to the test by Rob Gray . . .: Gray R, Beilock SL, 'Hitting is contagious: experience and action induction', *Journal of Experimental Psychology Applied*, vol. 17, no. 1, p. 49–59, 2011, pubmed.ncbi.nlm.nih.gov/21443380

p. 42　A 2012 study of batting averages since 1945 . . .: Bock JR, Maewal A & Gough DA, 'Hitting Is Contagious in Baseball: Evidence from Long Hitting Streaks', *PLoS One*, vol. 7, no. 12, 2012, www.ncbi.nlm.nih.gov/pmc/articles/PMC3520861

p. 42　In one study, researchers measured mirror neuron activity . . .: Fogassi L, 'Parietal Lobe: From Action Organization to Intention Understanding', *Science*, vol. 308, p. 662–7, 2005, doi.org/10.1126/SCIENCE.1106138

p. 43　Very recent research with baseball players . . .: Chen Y, Chang C & Huang S, 'Strike or ball? Batters know it better: an fMRI study of action anticipation in baseball players', *Cerebral Cortex*, vol. 33, no. 6, p. 3221–38, 2023, doi.org/10.1093/cercor/bhac271

p. 43   A batter has 0.4 seconds of ball flight time . . .: Willis F, 'The Science Behind Baseball', *SciJourner*, 2012, www.scijourner. org/2012/03/02/the-science-behind-baseball

p. 45   During 2021, Microsoft, the creator of . . .: Teevan J et al. (eds), *The New Future of Work 2022*, Microsoft Research Tech Report MSR-TR-2022-3, 2022, aka.ms/nfw2022

p. 47   We actually appear to feel the pain or disgust . . .: Morrison I et al., 'Vicarious responses to pain in anterior cingulate cortex: is empathy a multisensory issue?', *Cognition, Affective & Behavioural Neuroscience*, vol. 4, no. 2, p. 270–8, 2004, pubmed. ncbi.nlm.nih.gov/15460933; Wicker B et al., 'Both of us disgusted in My insula: the common neural basis of seeing and feeling disgust', *Neuron*, vol. 40, no. 3, p. 655–64, 2003, pubmed.ncbi. nlm.nih.gov/14642287

p. 47   In 2015, Keren Haroush from Stanford University . . .: Haroush K, Williams ZM, 'Neuronal Prediction of Opponent's Behavior during Cooperative Social Interchange in Primates', *Cell*, vol. 160, no. 6, p. 1233–45, 2015, doi.org/10.1016/j. cell.2015.01.045; Tian J, Uchida N, 'Monkeys in a Prisoner's Dilemma', *Cell*, vol. 160, no. 6, p. 1045–8, 2015, www. sciencedirect.com/science/article/pii/S0092867415002500

p. 49   Animals, including us, feel four basic emotions . . .: Izard EC, 'Basic Emotions, Natural Kinds, Emotion Schemas, and a New Paradigm', *Perspectives on Psychological Science*, vol. 2, no. 3, p. 260–80, 2007, https://doi.org/10.1111/j.1745-6916.2007.00044.x

p. 50   Humans are not the only species . . .: Banovac I, et al., 'Von Economo Neurons – Primate-Specific or Commonplace in the Mammalian Brain?', *Frontiers in Neural Circuits*, vol. 15, 2021, www.frontiersin.org/articles/10.3389/fncir.2021.714611/full

p. 51   They are also likely to be present . . .: Rogers NC et al., 'Oxytocin- and arginine vasopressin-containing fibers in the cortex of humans, chimpanzees, and rhesus macaques', *American Journal of Primatology*, vol. 80, no. 10, 2018, www.ncbi.nlm.nih. gov/pmc/articles/PMC6202198

p. 51   Adult humans have at least five times . . .: Allman JM, 'The von Economo neurons in fronto-insular and anterior cingulate cortex', *Annals of the New York Academy of Sciences Journal*, vol. 1225, p. 59–71, 2011, www.ncbi.nlm.nih.gov/pmc/articles/PMC3140770

p. 51 By eight months, we have . . .: Butti C et al., 'Von Economo neurons: Clinical and evolutionary perspectives', *Cortex*, vol. 49, no. 1, p. 312–16, 2013, doi.org/10.1016/j.cortex.2011.10.004

p. 52 You fail to acquire empathy and trust . . .: Ly M et al., 'Cortical thinning in psychopathy', *American Journal of Psychiatry*, vol. 169, no. 7, p. 743–9, 2012, www.ncbi.nlm.nih.gov/pmc/articles/PMC3815681

3 Psychopathy

p. 54 When he ran into computer science professor . . .: Shekhar C, 'Computer scientist fights spam on two fronts', *UC Santa Cruz: Baskin Engineering*, 2006, www.web.archive.org/web/20211215150733/https://engineering.ucsc.edu/news/article/1183

p. 54 Lee was an incredibly talented . . .: 'Our Story', *Cloudflare*, www.cloudflare.com/our-story

p. 54 Working for room and board . . .: Alspach K, 'Why Matthew Prince thinks AWS is Cloudflare's biggest security rival', *Protocol*, 2022, www.protocol.com/enterprise/cloudflare-matthew-prince-aws-cybersecurity

p. 56 In an interview with *Wired* magazine . . .: Upson S, 'The Devastating Decline of a Brilliant Young Coder', *Wired*, 2020, www.wired.com/story/lee-holloway-devastating-decline-brilliant-young-coder

p. 56 Kristin initially put Lee's behaviour . . .: 'Digital Biomarkers of FTD: How to Move from Tech Tinkering to Trials', *ALZForum*, 2022, www.alzforum.org/news/conference-coverage/digital-biomarkers-ftd-how-move-tech-tinkering-trials

p. 56 Pick's disease is the most common . . .: Pippin MM, Gupta V, 'Pick Disease', *StatPearls*, 2023, www.ncbi.nlm.nih.gov/books/NBK562226

p. 57 Examples from published case studies . . .: Cauda F, Geminiani GC & Vercelli A, 'Evolutionary appearance of von Economo's neurons in the mammalian cerebral cortex', *Frontiers in Human Neuroscience*, vol. 8, 2014, www.frontiersin.org/articles/10.3389/fnhum.2014.00104/full

p. 57 Glick has documented the course . . .: Glick H, *FTD/Dementia Support Blog*, earlydementiasupport.blogspot.com;: Glick H, 'Howard's Brain', *Kickstarter*, 2012, www.kickstarter.com/ projects/thinkfilm/howards-brain

p. 58 Early in the course of his disease . . .: Walton AG, 'Inside the Mind Of Frontotemporal Degeneration: A Patient's Story', *Forbes*, 2012, www.forbes.com/sites/alicegwalton/2012/05/09/ inside-the-mind-of-frontotemporal-degeneration-a-patients-story

p. 59 But this doesn't mean . . .: Ly M et al., 'Cortical thinning in psychopathy', *American Journal of Psychiatry*, vol. 169, no. 7, p. 743–9, 2012, www.ncbi.nlm.nih.gov/pmc/articles/PMC3815681

p. 59 In 1835, British physician . . .: Prichard JC, *A Treatise on Insanity and Other Disorders Affecting the Mind*, 1837, Haswell, Barrington and Haswell

p. 59 The term 'psychopath' caught on . . .: Skeem J, Polaschek D & Lilienfeld S, 'Psychopathic Personality', *Psychological Science in the Public Interest*, vol. 12, p. 162–95, 2011, doi.org/10.1177/1529100611426706

p. 61 As later researchers put it . . .: Johns JH, Quay HC, 'The effect of social reward on verbal conditioning in psychopathic and neurotic military offenders', *Journal of Consulting and Clinical Psychology*, vol. 26, p. 217–20, 1962, pubmed.ncbi.nlm.nih. gov/14451977

p. 62 In an article published . . .: Cleckley H, 'The So-Called Psychopathic Personality, With Special Emphasis on his Status in the Selective Service', *Journal of the Medical Association of Georgia*, vol. 30, p. 466–72, 1941, archive.org/stream/ journalofmedical3019medi/journalofmedical3019medi_djvu.txt

p. 63 The book was so popular . . .: American Psychiatric Association, *Diagnostic and statistical manual of mental disorders*, 1st edition, 1952, United States

p. 64 A major study of diagnostic consistency . . .: Spitzer, RL, Fleiss, JL, 'A re-analysis of the reliability of psychiatric diagnosis', *The British Journal of Psychiatry*, vol. 125, p. 341–7, 1974, doi.org/10.1192/bjp.125.4.341

p. 69 In one of his first trials . . .: Hare RD, 'Temporal gradient of fear arousal in psychopaths', *Journal of Abnormal Psychology*, vol. 70, no. 6, p. 442–5, 1965, doi.org/10.1037/h0022775

p. 70   In that trial, Hare asked . . .: Hare RD, Hart SD & Harpur TJ, 'Psychopathy and the *DSM-IV* criteria for antisocial personality disorder', *Journal of Abnormal Psychology*, vol. 100, no. 3, 1991, p. 391–8, psycnet.apa.org/record/1991-33364-001

p. 70   That, combined with their ability to charm . . .: Rice ME, Harris GT, 'Violent recidivism: assessing predictive validity', *Journal of Consulting and Clinical Psychology*, vol. 63, no. 5, p. 737–48, 1995, pubmed.ncbi.nlm.nih.gov/7593866

p. 70   By 1980, the year any semblance of psychopathy . . .: Hare RD, 'A research scale for the assessment of psychopathy in criminal populations', *Personality and Individual Differences*, vol. 1, no. 2, p. 111–19, 1980, www.sciencedirect.com/science/article/abs/pii/0191886980900288

p. 71   In 1991, Hare released . . .: Hare RD, Hart SD & Harpur TJ, 'Psychopathy and the *DSM-IV* criteria for antisocial personality disorder', *Journal of Abnormal Psychology*, vol. 100, no. 3, 1991, p. 391–8, psycnet.apa.org/record/1991-33364-001

p. 74   The PPI asks us to rate ourselves . . .: Lilienfield SO et al., 'PPI-R: Psychopathic Personality Inventory – Revised', *PAR*, www.parinc.com/Products?pkey=331

p. 74   Oxford University psychologist Kevin Dutton . . .: Wallis C, 'Of Psychopaths and Presidential Candidates', *Scientific American*, 2016, blogs.scientificamerican.com/mind-guest-blog/of-psychopaths-and-presidential-candidates; Dutton has created an online version of this test which you can try yourself. It can be found at: 'The Psychopath Challenge', 2020, www.drkevindutton.com/features/the-psychopath-challenge

p. 79   Kiehl found that connections . . .: Gregory S et al., 'The Antisocial Brain: Psychopathy Matters: A Structural MRI Investigation of Antisocial Male Violent Offenders', *JAMA Psychiatry*, vol. 69, no. 9, p. 962–72, 2012, jamanetwork.com/journals/jamapsychiatry/fullarticle/1149316

p. 80   Since 1948, psychologists have been . . .: Mueller S, 'Screenshots', *PEBL: The Psychology Experiment Building Language*, pebl.sourceforge.net/screenshots.html

p. 81   The test can be scored using . . .: Buchsbaum BR et al., 'Meta-analysis of neuroimaging students of the Wisconsin Card-Sorting task and component process', *Human Brain Mapping*, vol. 25, no. 1, p. 34–5, 2005, www.ncbi.nlm.nih.gov/pmc/articles/PMC6871753

p. 81   People with injury to the anterior . . .: Yang Y et al., 'Abnormal Structural Correlates of Response Perseveration in Individuals With Psychopathy', *Journal of Neuropsychiatry and Clinical Neurosciences*, vol. 23, no. 1, p. 107–10, 2011, www.ncbi.nlm. nih.gov/pmc/articles/PMC3197840

p. 82   More recently Kiehl has been using . . .: 'Psychopaths' brains show differences in structure and function', *University of Wisconsin-Madison School of Medicine and Public Health*, 2011, www.med.wisc.edu/news-and-events/2011/november/ psychopaths-brains-differences-structure-function; Motzkin JC, 'Reduced Prefrontal Connectivity in Psychopathy', *Journal of Neuroscience*, vol. 31, no. 48, p. 17348–57, 2011, www.ncbi.nlm. nih.gov/pmc/articles/PMC3311922

p. 82   These have confirmed that the tissue . . .: Espinoza FA et al., 'Resting-state fMRI dynamic functional network connectivity and associations with psychopathy traits', *NeuroImage: Clinical*, vol. 24, 2019, www.ncbi.nlm.nih.gov/pmc/articles/ PMC6728837; Hoppenbrouwers SS et al., 'White Matter Deficits in Psychopathic Offenders and Correlation with Factor Structure', *PLoS One*, vol. 8, no. 8, 2013, www.ncbi.nlm.nih. gov/pmc/articles/PMC3748110; For more information, see also: Hofhansel L et al., 'Morphology of the criminal brain: gray matter reductions are linked to antisocial behavior in offenders', *Brain Structure and Function*, vol. 225, p. 2017–28, 2020, link. springer.com/content/pdf/10.1007/s00429-020-02106-6.pdf

p. 82   A long series of functional MRI studies . . .: Murray L, Waller R & Hyde LW, 'A Systematic Review Examining the Link Between Psychopathic Personality Traits, Antisocial Behavior, and Neural Reactivity During Reward and Loss Processing', *Journal of Personality Disorders*, vol. 9, no. 6, p. 497–509, 2018, www.ncbi. nlm.nih.gov/pmc/articles/PMC7238432; Murray L et al., 'Reward-Related Neural Correlates of Antisocial Behavior and Callous-Unemotional Traits in Young Men', *Biological Psychiatry: Cognitive Neuroscience and Neuroimaging*, vol. 2, no. 4, p. 346–54, 2017, www.ncbi.nlm.nih.gov/pmc/articles/PMC5606223

p. 83   Psychopaths learn from neither rewards . . .: Hathaway B, 'Psychopaths can regret bad decisions – but don't learn from them (YaleNews)', *Yale University*, 2016, modlab.yale.edu/news/ psychopaths-can-regret-bad-decisions-dont-learn-them-yalenews

p. 83   They do not moderate their desire . . .: Finger EC et al.,
'Disrupted Reinforcement Signaling in Orbital Frontal Cortex
and Caudate in Youths with Conduct Disorder/Oppositional
Defiant Disorder and High Psychopathic Traits', *American
Journal of Psychiatry*, vol. 168, no. 2, p. 152–62, 2011,
www.ncbi.nlm.nih.gov/pmc/articles/PMC3908480

p. 86   The answer is that there are . . .: Reidy DE, Kearns MC & DeGue S,
'Reducing psychopathic violence: A review of the treatment
literature', *Aggressive and Violent Behavior*, vol. 18, no. 5, p.
527–38, 2013, www.ncbi.nlm.nih.gov/pmc/articles/PMC5868429

p. 87   No-one at Mendota believes . . .: Hagerty BB, 'When Your Child Is
a Psychopath', *The Atlantic*, 2017, www.theatlantic.com/magazine/
archive/2017/06/when-your-child-is-a-psychopath/524502

p. 88   Two years after release . . .: Caldwell M et al., 'Treatment
Response of Adolescent Offenders With Psychopathy Features',
Criminal Justice and Behaviour, vol. 33, p. 571–96, 2006,
doi.org/10.1177/0093854806288176

p. 91   He said, 'They had these . . .: Pasquini M, 'Donald Trump
Explains Why He Threw Paper Towels at Crowd in Puerto Rico:
"I Was Having Fun"', *People*, 2017, people.com/politics/donald-
trump-explains-why-he-threw-paper-towels-puerto-rico

p. 92   There were several photographers . . .: Blake A, 'This photo of
Trump's notes captures his empathy deficit better than anything',
Washington Post, 2018, www.washingtonpost.com/news/
the-fix/wp/2018/02/21/this-photo-of-trumps-notes-captures-his-
empathy-problem-better-than-anything

p. 93   It is, of course, much easier . . .: Hamilton RB, Newman JP, 'The
response modulation hypothesis: Formulation, development, and
implications for psychopathy', p. 80–93, 2018, in Patrick CJ,
Handbook of psychopathy, 2006, The Guilford Press

p. 94   He isolated the hormone responsible . . .: The word 'oxytoci'
comes from *oxutokia*, formed by the words ωχνξ *(oxus*, meaning
sudden) *and* τ or χ ox ξ *(tokos*, meaning childbirth), which means
rapid birth.

p. 95   It is transmitted into our bloodstream . . .: Chen S et al.,
'Morpho-Electric Properties and Diversity of Oxytocin Neurons
in Paraventricular Nucleus of Hypothalamus in Female and Male
Mice', *Journal of Neuroscience*, vol. 42, no. 14, p. 2885–904,
2022, doi.org/10.1523/JNEUROSCI.2494-21.2022

p. 95   Oxytocin became interesting . . .: Magon N, Kalra S, 'The orgasmic
history of oxycotin: Love, lust, and labor', *Indian Journal of
Endocrinology and Metabolism*, vol. 15, no. 3, p. 156–61, 2011,
www.ncbi.nlm.nih.gov/pmc/articles/PMC3183515

p. 95   Ninety-seven per cent of mammal species . . .: Fraley RC,
Brumbaugh CC & Marks MJ, 'The Evolution and Function Of
Adult Attachment: A Comparative and Phylogenetic Analysis',
Journal of Personality and Social Psychology, vol. 89 no. 5,
p. 731–46, doi.org/10.1037/0022-3514.89.5.751

p. 96   When researchers have blocked . . .: Winslow JT et al., 'A role
for central vasopressin in pair bonding in monogamous prairie
voles', *Nature*, vol. 365, no. 6446, p. 545–8, 1993, pubmed.ncbi.
nlm.nih.gov/8413608

p. 97   When nasal sprays containing oxytocin . . .: Gedeon T, Parry J
& Völlm B, 'The Role of Oxytocin in Antisocial Personality
Disorders: A Systematic Review of the Literature', *Frontiers in
Psychiatry*, vol. 10, p. 76, www.ncbi.nlm.nih.gov/pmc/articles/
PMC6400857; Neto ML et al., 'Oxytocin and vasopressin
modulation of prisoner's dilemma strategies', *Journal of
Psychopharmacology*, vol. 34, no. 8, p. 891–900, www.ncbi.nlm.
nih.gov/pmc/articles/PMC7583454

p. 97   When researches have administered . . .: ibid.

p. 97   Their presence stimulates dopamine . . .: Love TM, 'Oxytocin,
Motivation and the Role of Dopamine', *Pharmacology
Biochemistry and Behavior*, vol. 119, p. 46–60, 2013,
doi.org/10.1016%2Fj.pbb.2013.06.011

p. 97   There is now a fast-expanding field . . .: Potretzke S,
Ryabinin AE, 'The Prairie Vole Model of Pair-Bonding and Its
Sensitivity to Addictive Substances', *Frontiers in Psychology*,
vol. 10, 2019, www.frontiersin.org/articles/10.3389/fpsyg.2019.
02477; Heinrichs M, Domes G, 'Neuropeptides and social
behaviour: effects of oxytocin and vasopressin in humans',
Progress in Brain Research, vol. 170, p. 337–50, 2008, pubmed.
ncbi.nlm.nih.gov/18655894

p. 97   Although the outcomes of that research . . .: Nave G, Camerer C
& McCullough M, 'Does Oxytocin Increase Trust in Humans?
A Critical Review of Research', *Perspectives of Psychological
Science*, vol. 10, no. 6, p. 772–89, 2015, pubmed.ncbi.nlm.nih.
gov/26581735

p. 98   And sometimes they even seem . . .: Cardoso C, Ellenbogen MA, Linnen A, 'The effect of intranasal oxytocin on perceiving and understanding emotion on the Mayer-Salovey-Caruso Emotional Intelligence Test (MSCEIT)', *Emotion*, vol. 14, no. 1, 2014, pubmed.ncbi.nlm.nih.gov/24188065

p. 98   Like humans, prairie voles . . .: Rogers CN et al., 'Oxytocin- and arginine vasopressin-containing fibers in the cortex of humans, chimpanzees, and rhesus macaques', *American Journal of Primatology*, vol. 80, no. 10, 2018, www.ncbi.nlm.nih.gov/pmc/articles/PMC6202198

p. 98   Imaging studies on prairie voles . . .: López-Gutiérrez MF et al., 'Brain functional networks associated with social bonding in monogamous voles', *eLife*, vol. 10, 2021, elifesciences.org/articles/55081.pdf

p. 98   This is likely how these hormones . . .: Aoki Y, Yamasue H, 'Reply: Does imitation act as an oxytocin nebulizer in autism spectrum disorder?', *Brain: A Journal of Neurology*, vol. 138, no. 7, 2015, academic.oup.com/brain/article/138/7/e361/253241

p. 100 But a 2010 study showed . . .: DeWall CN et al., 'Acetaminophen Reduces Social Pain: Behavioral and Neural Evidence', *Psychological Science*, vol. 21, no. 7, p. 931–7, 2010, www.semel.ucla.edu/sites/default/files/publications/July%202010%20-%20Tylenol%20reduces%20social%20pain.pdf

p. 101 As paracetamol doses increase . . .: Mischkowski D, Crocker J & Way BM, 'From painkiller to empathy killer: acetaminophen (paracetamol) reduces empathy for pain', *Social Cognitive and Affective Neuroscience*, vol. 11, no. 9, p. 1345–53, 2016, www.ncbi.nlm.nih.gov/pmc/articles/PMC5015806

p. 102 In Australia, more than 60 per cent . . .: 'Panadol's continuing dominance proves a pain for competitors', *Roy Morgan*, 2019, www.roymorgan.com/findings/panadols-continuing-dominance-proves-a-pain-for-competitors

p. 102 The average US adult consumes . . .: 'The medications that change who we are', *BBC*, www.bbc.com/future/article/20200108-the-medications-that-change-who-we-are

p. 102 The Interpersonal Reactivity Index (IRI) . . .: 'Interpersonal Reactivity Index', *Eckerd College Department of Psychology*, www.eckerd.edu/psychology/iri

p. 103 In 2010, Sara Konrath . . .: Konrath S, 'Changes in dispositional empathy in American college students over time: a meta-analysis', *Personality and Social Psychology Review*, 2011, www.academia.edu/7139247/Changes_in_dispositional_ empathy_in_American_college_students_over_time_a_meta_ analysis

4 The key features of psychopathy
p. 111 Afterwards, he was gushing in his praise . . .: 'Lloyd George Meets Hitler (1936)', *Alpha History*, alphahistory.com/ nazigermany/lloyd-george-meets-hitler-1936
p. 112 Donald Trump's niece Mary . . .: Trump ML, *Too Much and Never Enough: How My Family Created the World's Most Dangerous Man*, 2022, Simon & Schuster
p. 113 This was not a unique experience . . .: Gibson G, Shepardson D, "It's like kumbaya': Trump's genial private meetings with CEOs jar with public attacks', *Reuters*, 2017, www.reuters.com/article/ us-usa-trump-companies-insight-idUSKBN16F18M
p. 113 One of the seminal works . . .: Drachman D, deCarufel A & Insko CA, 'The extra credit effect in interpersonal attraction', *Journal of Experimental Social Psychology*, vol. 14, no. 5, p. 458–65, 1978, www.sciencedirect.com/science/article/abs/ pii/0022103178900422
p. 115 In his 1999 biography . . .: Byrne JA, 'Working for the Boss From Hell', *Fast Company*, 2005, www.fastcompany. com/53295/working-boss-hell
p. 115 Dunlap seemed to enjoy firing people . . .: Deutschman A, 'Is Your Boss a Psychopath?', *Fast Company*, 2005, www. fastcompany.com/53247/your-boss-psychopath
p. 115 Almost a decade later . . .: Ronson J, 'Your Boss Actually Is a Psycho', *GQ*, 2015, www.gq.com/story/your-boss-is-a-psycho-jon-ronson
p. 116 In his autobiography . . .: Dunlap JA, Andelman B, *Mean Business: How I Save Bad Companies and Make Good Companies Great*, 1997, Simon & Schuster
p. 116 In 1981, he told *People* magazine . . .: McAdams DP, *The Strange Case of Donald Trump: A Psychological Reckoning*, 2020, Oxford University Press
p. 116 He held a variety of executive jobs . . .: Norris F, 'The Incomplete Résumé: A special report', *New York Times*,

2001, www.nytimes.com/2001/07/16/business/incomplete-resume-special-report-executive-s-missing-years-papering-over-past.html

p. 117 He'd lasted just two months . . .: Byron CM, *Testosterone Inc: Tales of CEOs Gone Wild*, 2004, Wiley

p. 117 Donald Trump, for example, persistently . . .: Reilly R, 'How and why President Trump cheats at golf – even when he's playing against Tiger Woods', *Golf*, 2019, golf.com/lifestyle/celebrities/how-why-president-trump-cheats-golf-playing-tiger-woods

p. 117 Bryan Marsal, chair of the . . .: ibid.

p. 118 The auditors found expenses . . .: Norris F, 'The lost years of Albert Dunlap', *Tampa Bay Times*, 2001, www.tampabay.com/archive/2001/07/18/the-lost-years-of-albert-dunlap

p. 118 Dunlap was fired within the year . . .: Norris F, 'The Incomplete Résumé: A special report', *New York Times*, 2001, www.nytimes.com/2001/07/16/business/incomplete-resume-special-report-executive-s-missing-years-papering-over-past.html; Guilliat R, 'Getting the job done, Dunlap-style', *Australian Financial Review*, 1991, www.afr.com/companies/getting-the-job-done-dunlap-style-19911122-k9wbv

p. 119 He fired a fifth of the staff . . .: Stanwick S, Stanwick P, 'Sunbeam Corporation: "Chainsaw Al" and the Quest for a Turnaround', *Auburn University Harbert College of Business*, webhome.auburn.edu/~stanwsd/sunbeam.html

p. 119 He told the Packers to stay . . .: Williams P, 'Al Dunlap's disgrace', 2001, *Australian Financial Review*, www.afr.com/politics/al-dunlaps-disgrace-20010721-j6zti

p. 119 David Brandon, the president of Valassis . . .: ibid.

p. 120 Dunlap's control strategies are common . . .: Boddy CR et al., 'Extreme managers, extreme workplaces: capitalism, organizations and corporate psychopaths', *Organization*, vol. 22, no. 4, p. 530–51, 2015, eprints.mdx.ac.uk/22171

p. 120 Boddy, a leading expert in corporate . . .: Boddy CR, 'Psychopathic Leadership: A Case Study of a Corporate Psychopath CEO', *Journal of Business Ethics*, vol. 145, p. 141–56, 2017, link.springer.com/article/10.1007/s10551-015-2908-6

p. 121 He then ditched three-quarters . . .: Donway R, 'Al Dunlap: An Insider's View', *The Atlas Society*, 1997, www.atlassociety.org/

post/al-dunlap-an-insiders-view (reprinted from *Navigator* vol. 1, no. 4)

p. 122 After the purchase, the buyer . . .: Williams P, 'Al Dunlap's disgrace', 2001, *Australian Financial Review*, www.afr.com/ politics/al-dunlaps-disgrace-20010721-j6zti

p. 122 Sunbeam managers described . . .: Byrne JA, 'Chainsaw Al executes his business', *Australian Financial Review*,1999, www.afr.com/politics/chainsaw-al-executes-his-business-19991101-k94h9

p. 123 Al's time with Max Phillips . . .: Norris F, 'The Incomplete Résumé: A special report', *New York Times*, 2001, www. nytimes.com/2001/07/16/business/incomplete-resume-special-report-executive-s-missing-years-papering-over-past.html

p. 124 In the 2014 edition of his autobiography . . .: Sandomir R, 'Albert J. Dunlap, Tough Executive Known as Chainsaw Al, Dies at 81', *New York Times*, 2019, www.nytimes.com/2019/02/05/ obituaries/al-dunlap-dead.html

p. 125 Boddy's UK charity psychopath CEO thought . . .: Boddy CR, 'Psychopathic Leadership: A Case Study of a Corporate Psychopath CEO', *Journal of Business Ethics*, vol. 145, p. 141–56, 2017, link.springer.com/article/10.1007/s10551-015-2908-6

p. 126 He worked up options for the paint . . .: Wagner J, 'Trump shares mock-ups of new Air Force Ones featuring colors remarkably similar to his private jet', *Washington Post*, 2019, www.washingtonpost.com/politics/trump-shares-mock-ups-of-a-new-air-force-one-featuring-colors-remarkably-similar-to-his-private-jet/2019/06/13/945b9c50-8dc3-11e9-adf3-f70f78c156e8_story.html

p. 126 He obsessed over the design . . .: Frazin R, 'Trump wants border wall black, pointed: report', *The Hill*, 2019, thehill.com/ homenews/administration/444244-trump-wants-border-wall-to-be-black-pointed-report

p. 127 Trump replied, 'I got it . . .: Swan J, Talev M, 'Scoop: Trump suggested nuking hurricanes to stop them from hitting U.S.', *Axios*, 2019, www.axios.com/2019/08/25/trump-nuclear-bombs-hurricanes

p. 127 The idea wasn't original . . .: Strauss M, 'Nuking Hurricanes: The Surprising History of a Really Bad Idea', *National*

Geographic, 2016, www.nationalgeographic.com/science/article/
hurricanes-weather-history-nuclear-weapons

p. 127 Blanche Sprague, a high-ranking . . .: Laughland O, 'Ex-Trump
workers describe egocentric micromanager: 'Donald loves
Donald'", *Guardian*, 2016, www.theguardian.com/us-news/2016/
mar/14/donald-trump-former-employee-interviews-ego-diversity

p. 128 The call had been arranged . . .: Lee CE, Kube C, 'Chaos in
Syria, Washington after Trump call with Erdogan unleashed
Turkish military', *NBC News*, 2019, www.nbcnews.com/
politics/national-security/chaos-syria-washington-after-trump-
call-erdogan-unleashed-turkish-military-n1063516

p. 129 They had to destroy their own . . .: Loanes E, 'US troops
bombed their own anti-ISIS headquarters as Turkey-backed
fighters closed in during Trump's hasty retreat', *Business
Insider*, 2019, www.businessinsider.com/us-bombed-its-anti-isis-
headquarters-as-turkish-troops-advanced-2019-10

p. 130 In response, then Secretary of Defense . . .: Youssef NA,
Lubold G, 'Mattis, Blindsided by Trump's Syria Decision,
Resigned Days Later', *Wall Street Journal*, 2018, www.wsj.com/
articles/mattis-blindsided-by-trumps-syria-decision-resigned-
days-later-11545446308

p. 130 In one impulsive moment . . .: Singh M, 'Trump defends Syria
decision by saying Kurds "didn't help us with Normandy"',
2019, *Guardian*, www.theguardian.com/us-news/2019/oct/09/
trump-syria-kurds-normandy

p. 130 Democratic Senator Jack Reed . . .: Sanger DE, *New York Times*,
'Trump Followed His Gut on Syria. Calamity Came Fast.',
New York Times, 2019, www.nytimes.com/2019/10/14/world/
middleeast/trump-turkey-syria.html

p. 130 He went on to say that . . .: Johnson A et al., 'U.S. prepares to
withdraw from northern Syria before Turkish operation', *NBC
News*, 2019, www.nbcnews.com/news/world/u-s-says-it-will-
stand-aside-turkey-moves-syria-n1063106

p. 130 Trump acknowledged he was . . .: Associated Press, 'Trump
Says He's an "Island of One" on Syria', *U.S. News*, 2019,
www.usnews.com/news/world/articles/2019-10-12/trump-says-
hes-an-island-of-one-on-syria

p. 130 He thought it was a 'strategically . . .: Balz D, 'Trump's decisions
on Syria bear all the hallmarks of his "America First" foreign

policy', *Washington Post*, 2019, www.washingtonpost.com/
politics/trumps-decisions-on-syria-bear-all-the-hallmarks-of-his-
america-first-foreign-policy/2019/10/14/99e31242-eec7-11e9-
89eb-ec56cd414732_story.html

pp. 130–1 After his first meeting with . . .: Sanger DE, *New York Times*,
'Trump Followed His Gut on Syria. Calamity Came Fast.',
New York Times, 2019, www.nytimes.com/2019/10/14/world/
middleeast/trump-turkey-syria.html

p. 131 Chainsaw Al told Jon Ronson . . .: Ronson J, 'Your Boss Actually
Is a Psycho', *GQ*, 2015, www.gq.com/story/your-boss-is-a-
psycho-jon-ronson

p. 132 That meant for Trump, a year out . . .: Kim SM, Dawsey J,
'Unswayed by top advisors, Trump doubles down on decision to
withdraw troops', *Washington Post*, 2019, www.washingtonpost.
com/politics/unswayed-by-top-advisers-trump-doubles-down-on-
decision-to-withdraw-troops/2019/10/13/3305b884-edfc-11e9-
b2da-606ba1ef30e3_story.html

p. 133 This is the so-called trolley problem . . .: Foot P, 'The Problem
of Abortion and the Doctrine of the Double Effect', *Oxford
Review*, vol. 5, p. 5–15, 1967, philpapers.org/rec/FOOTPO-2

p. 134 In 2007, a team of researchers . . .: Koenigs M et al., 'Damage
to the prefrontal cortex increases utilitarian moral judgements',
Nature, vol. 446, no. 7138, p. 908–11, 2007, www.ncbi.nlm.nih.
gov/pmc/articles/PMC2244801

p. 138 In Boddy's study of the psychopathic CEO . . .: Boddy CR,
'Psychopathic Leadership: A Case Study of a Corporate
Psychopath CEO', *Journal of Business Ethics*, vol. 145, p. 141–56,
2017, link.springer.com/article/10.1007/s10551-015-2908-6

p. 139 In 2010, Kent Kiehl set out to . . .: Ermer E, Kiehl KA,
'Psychopaths are impaired in social exchange and precautionary
reasoning', *Psychological Science*, vol. 21, no. 10, p. 1399–405,
2010, www.ncbi.nlm.nih.gov/pmc/articles/PMC3042879

p. 139 These tasks, developed in the 1960s . . .: Wason PC, 'Reasoning',
New Horizons in Psychology, p. 135–51,1966, Penguin Books

p. 142 They feel fear, but don't perceive . . .: Hoppenbrouwers SS,
Bulten BH & Brazil IA, 'Parsing Fear: A Reassessment of the
Evidence for Fear Deficits in Psychopathy', *Psychological
Bulletin*, vol. 142, no. 6, p. 573–600, 2016, www.apa.org/pubs/
journals/features/bul-bul0000040.pdf

p. 142 Donald Trump was the most litigious . . .: Penzenstadler N, Page S, 'Exclusive: Trump's 3,500 lawsuits unprecedented for a presidential nominee', *USA Today*, 2016, www.usatoday.com/story/news/politics/elections/2016/06/01/donald-trump-lawsuits-legal-battles/84995854

p. 142 As his aides told the *New York Times* . . .: Baker P, 'The Story So Far: Where 6 Investigations into Donald Trump Stand', *New York Times*, 2022, www.nytimes.com/2022/09/19/us/politics/donald-trump-investigations.html

p. 143 He told them to draft . . .: ibid.

p. 145 He was so unhappy with . . .: Zotto B, 'What color was "Apple Beige"?', *Medium*, 2021, bzotto.medium.com/what-color-was-apple-beige-acd14bca0c1a

p. 145 He would regularly berate . . .: Tate R, 'What Everyone Is Too Polite to Say About Steve Jobs', *Gawker*, 2011, www.gawker.com/5847344/what-everyone-is-too-polite-to-say-about-steve-jobs

p. 146 He later told his biographer . . .: Isaacson W, *Steve Jobs*, 2021, Simon & Schuster; Smith D, 'The Steve Jobs guide to manipulating people and getting what you want', *Sydney Morning Herald*, 2018, www.smh.com.au/business/workplace/the-steve-jobs-guide-to-manipulating-people-and-getting-what-you-want-20181024-p50bkc.html

p. 146 To defuse the situation . . .: Seibold C, 'February 19, 1981: Jef Writes a Career Limiting Memo', *Apple Matters*, 2011, www.applematters.com/article/february-19-1981-jef-writes-a-career-limiting-memo

p. 146 In 1979, Jef Raskin . . .: Baer D, 'Here's the angry memo that Macintosh's original developer sent to Apple after Steve Jobs forced him out', *Business Insider*, 2015, www.businessinsider.com/jef-raskin-steve-jobs-firing-memo-2015-3#; Dormehl L, 'Today in Apple history: Mac creator complains about Steve Jobs', *Cult of Mac*, 2019, www.cultofmac.com/529187/mac-creator-jef-raskin-disses-steve-jobs

p. 146 Referring to his dictatorial style . . .: Grossman L, Mccracken H, 'The Inventor of the Future', *TIME*, 2011, content.time.com/time/subscriber/article/0,33009,2096294-3,00.html

p. 146 It is a primal method of communication . . .: Blair RJR, 'Facial expressions, their communicatory functions and neuro-cognitive substrates', *Philosophical Transactions of the Royal Society*, vol. 358, p. 561–72, 2003, www.ncbi.nlm.nih.gov/pmc/articles/PMC1693136/pdf/12689381.pdf

p. 147 When our behaviour causes distress . . .: Blair RJR, 'Traits of empathy and anger: implications for psychopathy and other disorders associated with aggression', *Philosophical Transactions of the Royal Society of London: Biological Sciences*, vol. 373, no. 1744, 2018, www.ncbi.nlm.nih.gov/pmc/articles/PMC5832681

p. 149 He said by the early 1980s . . .: Taylor J, 'Books and Business; Zen and the Art of Computing', *New York Times*, 1987, www.nytimes.com/books/99/01/03/specials/butcher-millionaire.html

p. 149 In later interviews he noted . . .: Gibbs S, 'Steve Wozniak: No one wanted to work under Steve Jobs ever again', *Guardian*, 2014, www.theguardian.com/technology/2014/jul/08/steve-wozniakr-steve-jobs-apple

p. 150 Al Dunlap was mean, ill-tempered . . .: 'Exit bad guy', *The Economist*, 1998, www.economist.com/business/1998/06/18/exit-bad-guy

p. 151 As one former National Security Council . . .: Toosi N, 'Trump's NSC rocked by Ukraine scandal', *Politico*, 2019, www.politico.com/news/2019/10/05/trumps-national-security-council-ukraine-030564

p. 152 Like Dunlap, Jobs blamed . . .: Jobs S, '"You've got to find what you love," Jobs Says', *Stanford News*, 2005, news.stanford.edu/2005/06/12/youve-got-find-love-jobs-says

9 Psychopath wrangling

p. 206 The *Washington Post* fact-checking department . . .: Kessler G, Rizzo S & Kelly M, 'Trump's false or misleading claims total 30,573 over 4 years', *Washington Post*, 2021, www.washingtonpost.com/politics/2021/01/24/trumps-false-or-misleading-claims-total-30573-over-four-years

p. 207 When Canadian Prime Minister . . .: Kambhampaty AP, Carlisle M & Chan M, 'Justin Trudeau Wore Brownface at 2001 "Arabian Nights" Party While He Taught at a Private School', *TIME*, 2019, time.com/5680759/justin-trudeau-brownface-photo

p. 208   When Donald Trump refused . . .: Nelson L, '"Grab 'em by the pussy": how Trump talked about women in private is horrifying', *Vox*, 2016, www.vox.com/2016/10/7/13205842/trump-secret-recording-women

p. 222   Fedmart had been created . . .: Zweibac E, '2012 Hall of Fame: Sol Price', *Supermarket News*, 2012, www.supermarketnews.com/people-awards/2012-hall-fame-sol-price

p. 224   Much later, Jim credited Sol . . .: 'James D. Sinegal, 1936–', *Reference for Business*, www.referenceforbusiness.com/biography/S-Z/Sinegal-James-D-1936.html

pp. 224–5 Sol wasn't happy to see him leave . . .: Boyle M, 'Why Costco is so addictive', *CNN Money*, 2006, money.cnn.com/magazines/fortune/fortune_archive/2006/10/30/8391725/index.htm

p. 226   Had you invested $1000 . . .: 'Costco – 37 Year Stock Price History | COST', *Macrotrends*, www.macrotrends.net/stocks/charts/COST/costco/stock-price-history

p. 226   They think Costco is too generous . . .: Allison M, 'Costco's colorful CEO, co-founder Jim Sinegal to retire', *Seattle Times*, 2011, www.seattletimes.com/business/costcos-colorful-ceo-co-founder-jim-sinegal-to-retire

p. 226   The wages are relatively high . . .: Greenhouse S, 'How Costco Became the Anti-Walmart', *New York Times*, 2005, www.nytimes.com/2005/07/17/business/yourmoney/how-costco-became-the-antiwalmart.html

p. 227   As Jim told *Ethix* magazine . . .: Erisman A, 'James D. Sinegal: A Long-Term Business Perspective in a Short-Term World', *Ethix*, 2003, ethix.org/2003/04/01/a-long-term-business-perspective-in-a-short-term-world

p. 228   The study took over seven years . . .: Kiel F, *Return on Character: The Real Reason Leaders and Their Companies Win*, 2015, Harvard Business Review Press

p. 229   At the other end of the scale . . .: Kiel F, 'Psychopaths in the C-suite', *TEDxBGI*, video, Youtube, 5 February 2013, www.youtube.com/watch?v=vqBPZR63vfA

Conclusion

p. 236   This was quite the achievement for a man . . .: Johnston I, 'Death of a despot, buffoon and killer', *The Scotsman*, 2003, www.scotsman.com/news/world/death-of-a-despot-buffoon-and-killer-2512319

p. 240 Murphy found that the isolated group . . .: Murphy JM,
'Psychiatric Labeling in Cross-Cultural Perspective', *Science*,
vol. 191, no. 4231, p. 1019–28, 1976, www.science.org/
doi/10.1126/science.1251213

p. 241 In January 2022, Dominic Cummings . . .: Cochrane A,
'Partygate: Met police give "damning" evidence to Sue
Gray probe', *The National*, 2022, www.thenational.scot/
news/19869844.partygate-met-police-give-damning-evidence-
sue-gray-probe

Index

MORE BY DAVID GILLESPIE

Taming Toxic People

'I didn't know how to deal with the poisonous and toxic people in my life or why they behaved the way they did, so I went looking for an answer. This book is what I found.'

Bestselling author David Gillespie turns his attention to a phenomenon that damages businesses, seeds mental disease and discomfort and can bring civilisations to the brink of implosion – the psychopath.

Psychopaths are often thought of as killers and criminals, but actually five to ten per cent of people are probably psychopathic without ever indulging in a single criminal act. These everyday psychopaths may be charming in the early stages of relationships or employment but, Gillespie argues, their presence in your life is at best disruptive, and at worst highly dangerous: they will leave you feeling cheated and humiliated, dominating and manipulating you to the point where you question your sanity. Worse, he cautions, at a societal level their tendency to gravitate towards positions of power can be disastrous.

Taming Toxic People is a practical guide to restraining that difficult person in your life, be it your boss, your spouse or a parent. But it is also a serious and meticulously researched warning: if we value a free and well-functioning society, we need to rebuild the sense of community that has historically kept the everyday psychopath in check, and we must understand and act to manage the psychopathic behaviour in our midst.